Helen Bower

Textiles at Temple Newsam

The Roger Warner Collection

Financial assistance for research and publication
has been received from:

The Museums & Galleries Commission
(Jerwood / MGC Cataloguing Grants Scheme)

The Leeds Art Collections Fund

The Pilgrim Trust

The Paul Mellon Centre for Studies in British Art,
London

The Marc Fitch Fund

The Aurelius Charitable Trust

The Decorative Arts Trust of Philadelphia, USA

The Yorkshire & Humberside Museums Council

Published by the Leeds Art Collections Fund
for Leeds Museums and Galleries

ISBN 0 901981 66 4

Design Groundwork, Skipton

Printed in England

Contents

Preface

This catalogue is the fourth in a series devoted to the collections of the decorative arts at Temple Newsam and Lotherton Hall. Previous catalogues have covered Leeds Creamware and other English Pottery (1976), Furniture (in three volumes, 1978 and 1998) and British Silver (1992). Although it differs in being a paperback book, very fully illustrated in colour, its purpose is the same: to make accessible to the public information about the collections of the decorative arts, whose national importance was recognised by the award of Designated status by the Museums & Galleries Commission in June 1997.

The collection of textiles accumulated by Roger Warner and given by him over a period of several years from 1985 onwards is kept entirely at Temple Newsam. This is fitting, because the textiles that had made up the dress of the Ingram, Meynell Ingram and Wood families, and their furnishings at Temple Newsam, were dispersed in a seven day sale in 1922, shortly before the house was given to Leeds by the Hon. Edward Wood, later Lord Halifax. The majority of Roger Warner's textiles were once dress fabrics or furnishings belonging to other great country houses and were acquired by him at auctions during his fifty-year career as an antique dealer.

The catalogue has been researched and written by Helen Bower, Assistant Curator at Temple Newsam. She has also photographed every single object (with the exception of the linen damasks which were photographed by Richard Littlewood). Because of the comprehensive nature of the collection, she could not have completed the catalogue without the expert advice of many leading textile specialists. They include past and present members of staff of the Victoria and Albert Museum in London: Rosemary Crill in the Indian and South-East Asian Department, Clare W. Browne, Wendy Hefford, Jennifer Wearden and Santina Levey in the Department of Textiles and Dress. The last-named, formerly Keeper of the Department, has been outstandingly generous with her knowledge, time and again saving us from errors of fact; we owe her an enormous debt of gratitude. Needless to say, none of these individuals, nor the many other historians and archivists who have helped – amongst them, John Cornforth, Margaret Driver, Denis Irwin of Stead McAlpin & Company Limited, Freddie Launert of Sanderson and Company, David Mitchell and Mary Schoeser – are responsible for any errors that remain in the catalogue. For additional help of various kinds we are most grateful to Roger and Ruth Warner, David and Elizabeth Bower, Betty Evans, Diana Grey, Beverley Silverman, Elizabeth Thackrah and Barbara Walker.

Finally we would particularly like to thank those bodies who have made this catalogue possible by providing generous grant-aid for research and publication: the Museums & Galleries Commission (through the Jerwood / MGC Cataloguing Grants Scheme), The Pilgrim Trust, the Paul Mellon Centre for Studies in British Art, the Marc Fitch Fund, the Aurelius Charitable Trust, the Decorative Arts Trust, the Yorkshire & Humberside Museums Council, the Tom Ingram Fund, and the Abegg-Stiftung, Bern, Switzerland.

James S. Fox
Chairman of the Leeds Art Collections Fund

Anthony Wells-Cole
Senior Curator, Temple Newsam House

Introduction

If there is one thing more fascinating than a truly eclectic collection, it is the collector behind it. Roger Warner is such a man. He has, as he puts it, 'an eye for the one-off'. During his fifty or so years in the antiques trade he bought, sold and kept an array of treasures worthy of the most curious of cabinets of curiosities. His taste for the more vernacular style of the late 17th and 18th centuries was not fashionable amongst his contemporaries, with whom the Regency style was enjoying a revival, and his alternative view was refreshing for those wanting something more distinctive. He did not buy objects simply for being decorative, having a very keen sense of their value as historical documents, and so a visitor to his shop could hope to see virtually anything, so long as it was out of the ordinary.

Roger Harold Metford Warner was born of a Quaker family in 1913, in Yorkshire. His father died of scarlet fever two months before he was born, and he was brought up by his mother and his uncles. Because of illness from the age of eleven he was educated at home, giving him the opportunity to develop interests which perhaps he might not have done otherwise. However, when he was eighteen he heard a lecture on furniture at the Victoria & Albert Museum, given by a public lecturer Fred Wilson, and became fascinated by the subject. After spending three winters in London studying with Mr Wilson, in 1936 he and his mother set up an antique shop on the High Street of Burford, Oxfordshire, where it was to remain for the next fifty years.

In a way he was very fortunate at the start of his career, for he was looking for objects to buy during a rather sad period of country house history. The post-war years saw the demise of the English country house as it once had been. Devastated by death duties, in an age which viewed the aristocratic lifestyle rather differently from times gone by, one by one the owners of some of the great houses of England sold up lock, stock and barrel; often the contents of such places had not been disturbed for centuries. Generations of heirlooms were scattered far and wide, never to meet again. It was at these unforgettable sales that Roger came by some of his most interesting and unusual pieces, and in many cases, saved them from disappearing altogether.

Roger and Ruth Warner, May 1997 (Simon Warner)

Until relatively recently, textiles were not considered to be of great monetary or historic value and so he was able to pick up wonderful furnishings and fragments, quite inexpensively, often as part of other lots. He sold the larger objects, such as tapestries and carpets, and kept the less saleable, but often more interesting things, for himself; he built up a vast and varied collection, including both dress and furnishing fabrics, many of which were once commonplace but are now – because they were never considered important enough to keep – rare survivals. At a sale at Wilton House he spotted an intriguing English knotted carpet (Cat. no. 183), unnoticed by others looking for more glamorous pieces, languishing in the bottom of a rather uninspiring painted deal cupboard. He subsequently bought the cupboard for a few pounds, just to have the carpet. He recollects that on another occasion as he was leaving, loading his car, he saw a porter manhandling a huge bundle of tatty-looking cloth into the sale-room. Catching a glimpse of brilliant yellow gleaming in its midst, he rushed back in, bid for the bundle and left with it. Five miles down the road, he stopped and unravelled the pile, mostly household stuff, until he revealed a sumptuous Queen Anne yellow silk needlework counterpane, screwed up in a ball.

Metford Warner

Country house sales were one source of his collection. The other was the textiles Roger inherited from his uncle and grandfather.

In 1872 his grandfather, Metford, had become the sole owner of the highly respected wallpaper manufacturing company *Jeffrey & Co.*, which specialized in producing *specimens of works of art in paper Decoration which display the highest and finest taste*. He took the company in hand, revolutionising the British wallpaper industry by refusing to accept that the only source of original designs for wallpaper was France, a belief which was reflected by contemporary public taste. Metford employed the designer Owen Jones and the architects Charles Eastlake, William Burges and Edward W. Godwin to produce him a set of designs for wallpapers which in 1873 won a medal at the London Annual International Exhibition.

In the following years he went on to use the work of many of the best known designers of the day, including C.F.A.Voysey, Lewis F. Day, Walter Crane, and Bruce J. Talbert; he himself was also an excellent draughtsman. Metford, like many of his contemporaries, was hugely influenced by the philosophy of William Morris, and the company had the honour of producing all Morris's designs for wallpapers, using the hand-block printing methods revived by him.

In 1911 Metford and his wife Agnes travelled in Italy and an entry in his sketchbook contains three useful phrases written out in English (with, he noted, Italian translations provided by the ABDC Translations Bureau):

Sir, I shall esteem it a great favour if you will permit me to photograph & make a drawing of the Silk Draperies which hang on the walls of your Church

Sir, I shall esteem it a great favour if you will allow me to see any ancient Silk or Velvet Vestments or Draperies which you may have in connection with your Church

Sir, Have you for sale any small or large pieces of Velvets or Silks which have been used for Church purposes such as Vestments or Draperies ? Wanted for Design only

He also made notes of some of the textiles he saw and bought and although these are tantalisingly brief it is certain that he did return with quantities of silk damasks and velvets, and an interesting group of linen and silk brocatelles, almost certainly made and used in Italy. His sons, Horace and Reginald were also collecting in the Low Countries around 1900 and whilst in Dordrecht bought Indian printed cotton bedspreads (now in the Indian section of the Victoria and Albert Museum) and other fragments, some of which are in this collection.

Metford's son, Reginald Warner performed a similar service to the world of weaving. He set up a hand-loom weaving company in Sudbury, Suffolk, where he had discovered a few remaining weavers. He provided them with premises, on the understanding that they would each take on an apprentice. The firm flourished, producing luxury fabrics in traditional designs, including, amongst many similar commissions, a red cotton damask for the Picture Gallery at Temple Newsam in 1940. The firm is still going strong under the name Gainsborough Silk Weaving Company and now has a vast range of designs to call upon.

Roger, like his grandfather, has a strong belief in the value of objects not just for their decorative element, but for what can be learnt from them about their design and manufacture. As a result he was and is extremely generous in giving such objects to museums in order to preserve them. It is this interest which makes the collection at Temple Newsam so significant: because he largely collected at country house sales, it provides a considerable amount of information about the huge variety of fabrics used in the different areas of a country house and how this has changed over the centuries.

There are several groups within the collection. Roughly a third is made up of silks, either for dress or furnishings, some of which are of silk combined with another fibre to create a heavier material. Since they cover a broad span from the late sixteenth to late nineteenth centuries they provide an overview of the development of pattern design. There is also a substantial number of printed cottons, again for both dress and furnishing, which illustrate technical progress in printing and dyestuffs, as well as a huge range of pattern types. A third group relates more specifically to furnishings, either pieces actually made up into furnishings, or heavyweight fabrics which could only have been used for that purpose. Especially useful are the pieces which remain made up – curtains, bed valances, case covers – for they indicate the sorts of materials thought appropriate for different uses, as well as the kinds of linings, trimmings and stitches employed. These details are invaluable when trying to re-create a historic interior.

Roger Warner Antiques. Front of shop premises, c. 1950

Textiles have always played a very important part in the decoration of an interior, by providing warmth, colour and comfort, as well as a certain flexibility in changing the appearance of a room. To keep out the draughts, bare walls, often un-plastered, were hung with tapestries or fabric, often panels of a heavy cloth woven from linen and silk, known as brocatelle. There are several examples of this fabric in the collection, from the late sixteenth to the nineteenth century, through which the development of a certain style of large scale foliate pattern can be traced. Mostly they are of a shade of red, occasionally red or green with yellow, and would have given a very rich, warm atmosphere to a room. The purpose of brocatelle was to imitate the more luxurious and less durable pure silk damask, of which there are also examples in this catalogue, which was used to cover walls in the best rooms of grand houses. In the case of both damasks and brocatelles, because of the difficulty and cost of re-hanging rooms and re-covering furniture, patterns remained current for decades, even for generations – indeed, the most popular patterns have been available from c.1700 (or earlier) to the present day.

During the eighteenth and nineteenth centuries furniture with decorative upholstery, such as velvet, damask, tapestry or needlework, was usually supplied with protective loose covers of linen or cotton or even leather; these were removed only for extremely important visitors. They are even illustrated in portraits, indicating how unusual it was for them to be taken off. The blue checked linen covers in the collection are typical. The set includes a bolster case, and long sofa cushion case, both of which retain the checked tape which neatens the seams, and a matching curtain, fitted with brass rings, attached with loops of the same checked tape. The sort of needlework upholstery which they might have preserved remains in its original form on three chairs illustrated here.

Beds were a focal point for the display of textiles. Wealthy people spent huge sums of money on the hangings (or *furniture*) for beds, which were seen as a status symbol. The furniture was often made from very luxurious and expensive fabrics, such as silk velvet and damask, with metal braids and trimmings. In the sixteenth and seventeenth centuries bed curtains of linen or fustian cloth, embroidered with wool or silk, were very fashionable, and there are fragments of these in the collection. There are also valances, probably not made for the grandest of beds, which on a four-post bed were used not only to hide the legs and the space under the bed but also hanging from the edge of the canopy to hide the curtain rail and rings. Like other furnishings they changed with fashion and these developments are reflected by the valances, from a late eighteenth century one of striped silk and linen, which is flat with a shaped lower edge, to early nineteenth century examples of gathered printed cotton, and Victorian ones of worsted in strong plain colours. Many of these have the original tapes and loops which were used to attach them to the bed frame and so are an invaluable in showing how the furniture of a bed fits together.

Wool fabrics form an unusually large part of the Roger Warner collection. Because of their more utilitarian nature, these tend to survive less well than the expensive fabrics but were in fact more widely used. Some are of a type known as moreen or harateen, made of worsted with a pattern stamped on it, rather than woven into it. In the eighteenth century the fashion for the arrangement of furniture in a room was very formal, with chairs standing against the wall, and this material was often used to cover the backs which were not usually seen. Also well represented is worsted damask, which the Victorians thought particularly suitable for bed and windows curtains, mostly in reds from brilliant scarlet to deep burgundy, often with patterns of small scattered sprigs of leaves or flowers. These are fascinating because many remain made up as curtains, retaining their rings and the patterned silk ribbon used to decorate the hem.

There are also a large number of dress fabrics in both silk and cotton. The fashion for patterns of multi-coloured silks was dictated by the silk designers, especially in the eighteenth century, and usually changed twice a year. These designs were created using a variety of complex weaves, worked on a hand-operated loom and the resulting materials were very expensive. Similar effects were achieved far more cheaply from the mid nineteenth century onwards, when the cost of silk thread had fallen and mechanised Jacquard looms (invented c.1801) had come into regular use.

Notes on the catalogue

The primary purpose of the catalogue is to provide a visual survey of the collection; a detailed technical analysis of individual pieces is not given. Within the colour section, the textiles are grouped in three categories according to the method used to create the pattern of the textiles, and then listed chronologically to show developments in pattern design.

Woven
Within the large woven section, the textiles are further sub-divided:

Multi-coloured silk fabrics, mainly for dress, in a variety of weaves; the captions indicate where, for instance, a textile is brocaded;

Damasks, and *Brocatelles*, fabrics in which the patterns changed relatively infrequently;

Wool, *Linen* and *Cotton* in various weaves;

Surface Finished fabrics, in which the pattern – dependent on texture and the play of light – has been achieved by various finishing techniques.

Printed and Painted
Fabrics, of various fibres, which have had colour applied by printing with a block, roller, or plate; or painting by hand using a very fine brush.

Embroidered
Textiles decorated with a variety of embroidery threads and techniques.

The colour section is followed by black and white illustrations of white linen damasks, and then by a list of textiles not illustrated.

Specimen catalogue entry

88 Woven silk [RW543]
Late 17th century
Damask
24½ × 22¼ (62.3 × 56.5) loom width;
P 30 est. × 11¼ (76 x 28.5)

88 is the catalogue number; **Woven silk** describes the type of fabric and fibre; **[RW543]** is the Roger Warner collection number.

The date, given as part of a century (unless it is known more precisely), is the earliest probable for the object illustrated.

An indication of the weave or method of decoration follows – in this case **damask**.

Dimensions of the object are in inches (centimetres in brackets), vertical before horizontal: where the full fabric width, including the selvedges, is known, this is noted as **loom width**; the pattern unit (**P**) is given where at least one dimension can be measured or estimated (**est**).

Woven

1 Furnishing or dress silk [RW1]
17th century
Cut and uncut pile velvet on satin ground
14 × 8
(35.5 × 21)
Maniple (part), lined with blue linen, trimmed with silver gilt bobbin lace (17th or 18th century).

2 Dress silk [RW43]
First half 17th century
Complex weave, lamé with silver gilt strip
22 × 12
(56 × 30.5);
P ? × 10¼ (26)

3 Furnishing and/or dress silk [RW4]
Mid 17th century design
Uncut pile velvet on satin ground
17¼ × 20¼
(43.7 × 51.4)
Mid 17th century pattern but probably later revival.

4 Dress silk [RW45]
Late 17th century
Complex weave
17 × 12
(43.2 × 30.5);
P 15¼ × 7¼
(38.8 × 18.5)

5 Dress silk [RW105]
Late 17th century
Complex weave brocaded with silk and gold filé
26 × 13¼ (66 × 33.7); P 2⅜ × 8⅜ (6 × 21.3)

6 Dress silk [RW365]
Late 17th century,
European for the Turkish market
Complex weave with brocading
23 × 15½
(96 × 39);
P 14½ × 4¼
(37 × 11)

Previous page: Dress silk, detail of Cat. no. 30 [RW537]

5 detail

7 detail

above
7 Woven silk
[RW44]
1670s to 90s
Complex weave
30 × 26
(76.2 × 66)
loom width
20 + selvedges;
P 14¾ × 10
(36.8 × 25.4)
Left selvedge.

left
8 Dress silk
[RW355]
1700 to 10
Damask
brocaded with
silk, silver and
silver gilt filé and
frisé
14¾ × 9¼
(38 × 23)

left
9 Dress silk
[RW81]
1705 to 10
Complex weave
brocaded with
silver filé and silk
24¼ × 8
(61.6 × 20.4)
Left selvedge.

right
10 Dress silk
[RW454]
Early 18th
century
Complex weave
26½ × 19½
(67.3 × 49.5);
P ? × 9¾ (27.3)
Cut and joined
for later use;
faded, originally
cream on mauve.

11 Dress silk
[RW78]
1710 to 20
Complex weave brocaded with gold and silver thread and silk
42 × 18¾ (106.7 × 47.7) loom width
Dress fabric re-used as a chasuble orphrey and maniple.

left
13 Dress silk
[RW49]
1720s
Complex weave
49 × 20½ (124.5 × 52) loom width; P 25 × 20 (63.5 × 50.8)
Possibly re-used as a humeral veil, a vestment worn over the shoulders.

below
14 Furnishing silk [RW54]
1720s
Complex weave
24¼ × 20¼ (61.6 × 51.4) loom width; P 18¾ × 20 (47.6 × 50.8)

above
12 Dress or furnishing silk
[RW80]
1710s
Complex weave brocaded with gold filé
9 × 8½ (22.8 × 21.6)

left
15 Dress silk
[RW58]
1725 to 35
Complex weave
42 × 9¾ (106.7 × 24.8)
loom width 20¾ (52.7); P 26¾ × 9⅜ (68 × 23.7)
Right selvedge.

16 Furnishing or dress silk [RW74]
1720s
Complex weave, the ground lamé with silver filé, brocaded in silk and gold filé
7½ × 19¾ (19 × 49.5) loom width

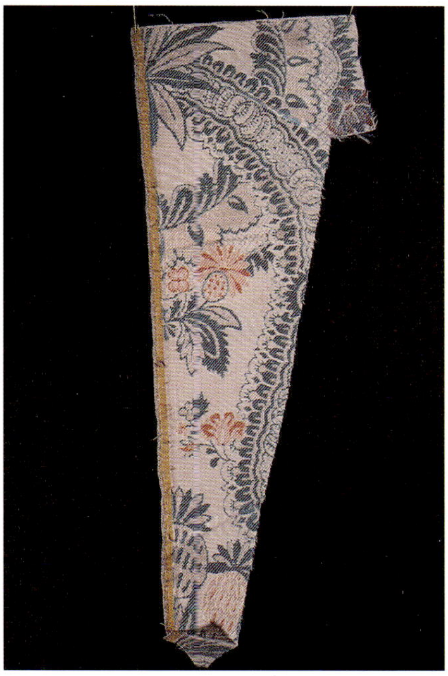

17 Dress silk
[RW361]
1720s
Complex weave
15 × 5¼
(37 × 13);
P 14 (35.5) × ?
One selvedge.

18 Woven silk [RW84]
1720s
Complex weave, brocaded damask
25 × 16¾ (63.5 × 42.6) loom width; P 17 × 8¼ (43.2 × 21)

19 Dress silk
[RW83]
Second quarter 18th century
Complex weave with brocading
28½ × 7
(72.4 × 17.8);
P 12⅜ (31.4) × ?

20 Furnishing silk [RW2 & 3]
Mid 18th century
Cut pile velvet on voided ground, with supplementary metal strip
19 × 17
(48 × 43.5)

above
22 Woven silk
[RW48]
20th century
based on Cat no.
21 [RW47]
Complex weave
21 × 21¾ (53.4 × 55.2); P 23½ × 21¼ (59.7 × 54)
Possibly
Gainsborough
Silk Weaving Co.

left
23 Woven silk
[RW60]
Mid 18th century
or later revival
Complex weave
39 × 21 (99 × 53.4) loom width; P 24¾ × 9½ (63 × 24)

above
21 Woven silk [RW47]
1730s
Complex weave
46 × 19¾ (107 × 50.2) loom width;
P 23½ × 19¼ (59.7 × 49)

right
24 Woven silk [RW61]
Mid 18th century
Complex weave
17½ × 19½ (44.5 × 49.5); P ? × 10¾ (27.3)

25 Dress silk [RW86]
1730s
Complex weave with brocading
11¾ × 20 (29.8 × 50.8) loom width; P ? × 19½ (49.6)

27 Woven silk [RW97]
1750s
Complex weave brocaded with silk and silver gilt strip and filé
43¾ × 9¾ (111 × 24.7); P 14¾ (37.5) × ?

left
26 Dress silk
[RW88]
1730s
Complex weave with brocading
15¾ × 5½
(40 × 14)

below left
28 Woven silk, ornament d'église [RW99]
Mid 18th century
Complex weave brocaded with silk and silver gilt filé
31½ × 20¼
(80 × 51.5);
P 14½ (36.8) × ?

right
29 Dress silk
[RW101]
Mid 18th century
Complex weave with brocading
18 × 21½
(45.8 × 54.6)
loom width;
P 17⅝ × 13¾
(44.7 × 34.9)
Design was originally filled out with a ground pattern in white silk, now largely missing.

30 Dress silk
[RW537]
Mid 18th century
Complex weave with cut and uncut pile velvet on a silver ground
15¾ × 12½ (40 × 31.7); P 6 × 6½ (15.2 × 16.5)
Used as a stomacher.
(Detail, p 1)
Bought Kelmscott Manor, Oxfordshire, sale, 1939
(? ex coll. William Morris)

31 Woven silk
[RW538]
Mid 18th century
Complex weave with brocading
11½ × 10¾ (29.2 × 27.8)
Bought Kelmscott Manor, Oxfordshire, sale, 1939
(? ex coll. William Morris)

below left
32 Dress silk
[RW85]
c.1735, probably French
Complex weave with brocading
9 × 9 (22.9 × 22.9)
Right selvedge.

right
33 Dress or furnishing silk
[RW89]
1735 to 45
Complex weave with brocading
43¼ × 11¼ (109.9 × 28.6); P 16¾ × 10¾ (42.5 × 27.3)
This silk imitates both the design and technical effects of contemporary English embroidery.
Right selvedge.

31 detail

34 Dress silk
[RW82]
1740s
Complex weave with brocading
24¾ × 11 (62.8 × 28);
P 8½ × 7 (21.7 × 17.8)

35 Furnishing silk [RW312]
1738
Cut and uncut pile velvet on satin ground
22 × 28⅜ (56 × 72); P ? × 21½ (54.6)
Represents the Hindu deity Siva. A room at Ditchley Park, Oxfordshire, is hung with the same silk. *Country Life*, 24 November 1988, p 84; Geoffrey Beard, *Upholsterers and Interior Furnishing in England 1530–1840* (New Haven and London, 1997), p.189, fig. 200.

36 Dress silk [RW93]
1740s
Complex weave with brocading
10½ × 21¾ (26.7 × 55.3) loom width; P ? × 10⅜ (26.4)
Re-used as a valance, probably in the 19th century.

37 Dress silk, 3 joined pieces [RW102]
1740s
Complex weave with brocading
16½ × 25 (42 × 63.5); P 13¼ (33.7) × ?

38 Dress silk
[RW461]
1740s
Complex weave with brocading
39½ × 16¼ (100.3 × 41.3) loom width;
P 18¾ × 15¾ (47.5 × 40)

35 detail

39 Woven silk
[RW94]
1750s to 60s
Complex weave brocaded with silver filé and strip
28¼ × 5⅝
(71.7 × 13.7);
P 20¼ (51.4) × ?

40 Dress silk
[RW100]
c.1750
Complex weave with brocading
14⅝ × 10⅜
(37 × 26.4)

41 Dress silk
[RW413]
1750s
Complex weave brocaded with silk and silver and gilt strip
50 × 20
(120 × 52) loom width;
P 19¼ × 10
(48 × 26)

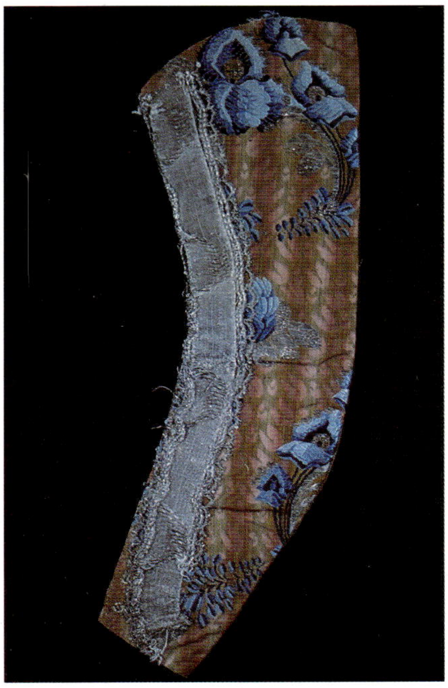

42 Dress silk
[RW455]
1750s to 60s
Complex weave brocaded with silk and silver filé and silver strip
16¾ × 6
(42.5 × 15.2)
Sleeve re-used for the robe of a devotional statue, with eyelet holes at cuff, and trimmed with silver braid and bobbin lace.

42 detail

43 **Woven silk** [RW457]
1750s
Complex weave with brocading
80½ × 41½ (204.5 × 105.5); P 17¾ × 10¾ (45 × 27.3)

44 **Woven silk**
[RW63]
Late 18th century
Complex weave
5½ × 20
(14 × 50.8);
P 3⅛ × 3½
(7.9 × 8.9)

45 **Woven silk** [RW65]
1760s to 70s
Complex weave
15½ × 21¼ (39.4 × 54) loom width;
P 4¾ × 10⅜ (12.1 × 26.4)

46 **Dress silk**
[RW92]
c.1760
Complex weave
with brocading
15¼ × 7¼
(38.7 × 18.4)

47 **Dress silk** [RW95 & 96]
1760s to 70s
Complex weave with brocading
23 × 22 (58.4 × 55.9); P 15 × 18 (38.1 × 45.7)

46 detail

48 Furnishing silk [RW284]
Late 18th century
Tabby weave
10½ × 65½ (26.7 × 166.3)
Pelmet or valance lined with heavy linen and bound with patterned silk and wool ribbon. Remains of a silk tassel on one corner.

below left
49 Furnishing silk [RW346]
Late 18th century
Complex weave
27½ × 31¾ (70 × 80.7); P ? × 9¼ (23.5)
Bourette. Cf. RW316 (Cat no.65). One selvedge.

left
51 Nine different dress silks [RW464]
Late 18th century
Complex weaves
4¼ × 4 × 9.5 (10.8 × 10.2 × 24.1) when open.
Purse or huswife containing a red baize needlecase edged with metal thread, and a length of cotton lace wrapped round a visiting card inscribed *John Ford/York*.

50 Dress silk [RW358–360]
c.1760
Complex weave
23¼ × 10½ (60 × 27); P 14¾ (37.5) × ?
Stud and nail marks indicate re-used for upholstery. Machine-seamed.

52 Dress silk [RW64]
1770s
Complex weave
16¼ × 9½ (41.3 × 24.2); P 2¾ × 5¾ (7 × 14.7)
Right selvedge.

left
53 Furnishing silk [RW91]
1770s to 80s
Complex weave with brocading
15 × 8¼ (38.2 × 21)
Colour & style of flowers suggests fragment of large scale French furnishing silk.

right
54 Dress silk [RW103]
1770s
Complex weave with brocading
21¾ × 10 (55.3 × 25.4); P 7 × 8⅝ (17.8 × 21.9)
Left selvedge.

55 Woven silk [RW459]
1770s
Tabby weave, painted and brocaded with silver gilt filé and silver strip
39 × 21¼ (99 × 54) loom width; P 4¾ × 10½ (12 × 26.7)
Originally in white and metal, but probably over-painted in the 19th or 20th century.

56 Dress silk [RW66]
1790s
Complex weave
26 × 10½ (66 × 26.7); P 5¾ × 7 (14.6 × 17.8)

57 Dress silk [RW68]
1790s
Complex weave
17 × 10¼ (43.2 × 26); P 1 × 8 (2.5 × 20.3)
One selvedge.

58 Woven silk [RW69]
Early 19th century
Complex weave
17½ × 21½ (44.5 × 54.6); P ? × 10¼ (25.9)

left
59 Woven silk
[RW70]
c.1800 to 10,
French
Complex weave
48¾ × 9½
(123.8 × 24.2);
P 47¼ (120) × ?

60 Furnishing silk [RW316]
Second half 18th century or 19th century
Twill weave
36 × 35 (91.5 × 89) loom width 18 (45.7); P ? × 6 (15.3)
Bourette.

right
61 Dress silk
[RW463]
c.1800
Tabby weave with
silver gilt strip
14¼ × 16
(36.2 × 40.6)
Possibly a
knotting bag,
trimmed with
cream silk fringe,
and draw
ribbons.

left
62 Woven silk
[RW450]
c.1812, French
Complex weave
55 × 23½
(139.7 × 59.7);
P 46¼ × 22¾
(117.5 × 58)
Cf. Jane C.
Nylander, *Fabrics for Historic Buildings*,
(Washington,
D.C., 1983) p.85;
Paris, Mobilier National Soieries Empire. Inventaire des collections publiques français,
(Paris, 1980),
p.112

63 Mixed silk and cotton furnishing [RW319]
Second half 19th century
Complex weave
16 × 21 (40.6 × 53.3) loom width 20½ (52);
P 5½ × 5 (14 × 12.7)
Stitch marks and soiling pattern indicate that it was originally part of buttoned chair upholstery.

left
65 Dress silk
[RW363]
c.1850
Complex weave with brocading
30 × 15¼ (70 × 39);
P 15 × 7½ (38 × 19)
Campbell, Harrison & Lloyd, c.1850

above
64 Dress silk
[RW356]
Third quarter 19th century
Complex weave
7⅞ × 8⅝ (20 × 22);
P c.8⅝ × 3¾ (22 × 9.5)
An avant garde design of its time.

left
66 Furnishing silk [RW418]
Late 19th century
Jacquard weave
80 × 20½ (200 × 52.5) loom width;
P 64 × 20 (163 × 52.5)
Inspired by mid 18th century design.

left
67 Dress silk
[RW427]
Late 19th century
Complex weave
25 × 11 (63.5 × 27.9);
P ? × 3¾ (9.5)

right
68 Mixed cotton and silk furnishing
[RW442]
Late 19th century
Jacquard weave
26 × 28 (66 × 71.1);
P 24 × 21¼ (61 × 54)

left
69 Dress silk
[RW451]
Late 19th century
Jacquard weave
42 × 22½
(106.7 × 57.7);
P 12¼ × 7½
(39 × 19)
Skirt panel.

right
70 Dress silk
[RW456]
Late 19th century
Complex weave
with brocading
22 × 21½
(56 × 54.6);
P ? × 10¼ (26)
Influenced by the
designs and
techniques of the
1770s.

72 Dress silk
[RW460]
Late 19th century
Complex weave
20 × 31
(50.8 × 79);
P 4 × 5½
(10 × 14)

above
71 Woven silk
[RW458]
Late 19th century
Jacquard weave
27 × 26
(68.6 × 66);
P 8½ × 6½
(21.5 × 16.5)
Left selvedge.

left
73 Dress silk
[RW462]
c.1881
Complex weave
9 × 5 (23 × 10.7);
P 6¼ × c.6
(16 × 15)
Fragment from a
Quaker wedding
dress.

74 Furnishing silk [RW71]
c.1900
Jacquard weave
37 × 24
(94 × 61);
P 17¾ × 25
(45.1 × 63.5)
Pastiche based on
earlier Oriental
and European
designs.

75 Dress silk [RW104]
Early 20th century close copy of 1770s silk
Complex weave with brocading
8⅝ × 21½ (22 × 54.6) loom width; P ? × 21½ (54.6)

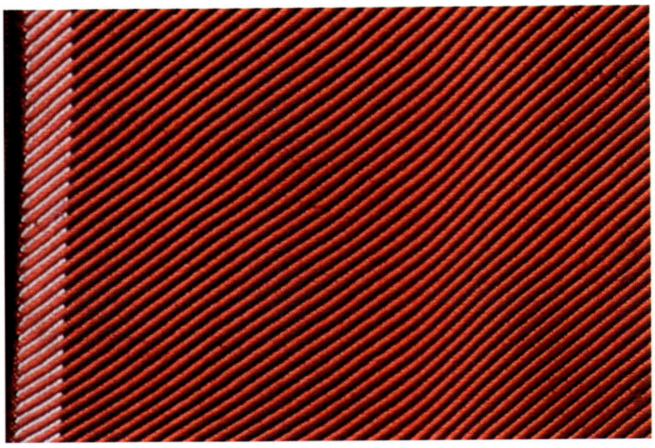

76 Woven silk [RW439]
20th century
Twill weave
21½ × 30 (54.6 × 76.2) loom width 21½ (54.6)

77 Dress silk [RW440]
Late 19th or early 20th century
Complex weave
59 × 34 (150 × 86.4); P 26½ × 32 (67.3 × 81.3)
The colouring of the flowers was achieved by dyeing the relevant areas of the warp before weaving, an effect known as *chiné*.

78 Furnishing silk [RW36]
c.1600
Damask
6½ × 15 (16.5 × 38); P 5¼ × 5½ (13.5 × 14)

79 Dress silk, 2 pieces [RW37]
Second quarter 17th century
Damask
24¾ × 15 (63 × 38);
P 23 × 5½ (58.5 × 14)

81 Dress or furnishing silk
[RW447]
Mid 17th century
Damask
43 × 22½
(109.2 × 57.2);
P 18½ × 11
(47 × 28)
Two strips joined vertically, each with one selvedge.

above
80 Dress silk
[RW10]
Mid 17th century
Damask
19½ × 20½
(49.5 × 52);
P 9 × 5½ (23 × 14)
Lined with pieces of pale blue linen.

left
82 Furnishing silk [RW6]
Third quarter 17th century
Damask
29¼ × 22½
(74 × 56)
loom width;
P 24¼ × 11
(61.5 × 28)

83 Furnishing or dress silk
[RW8]
Third quarter 17th century
Damask
21½ × 8¾
(54.6 × 22.2);
P ? × 5⅜ (13.7)

84 Dress silk
[RW9]
Second half of 17th century
Damask
36¼ × 27½
(92 × 70) loom width 22 (56);
P 20¼ × 10¾
(51.5 × 27.3)
Printed card attached of Reginald Warner, Gainsborough Silk Weaving Co., Sudbury, Suffolk.

85 Dress silk
[RW7]
Late 17th century
Damask
16¼ × 8¼
(42.5 × 21);
P ? × 7 (18)

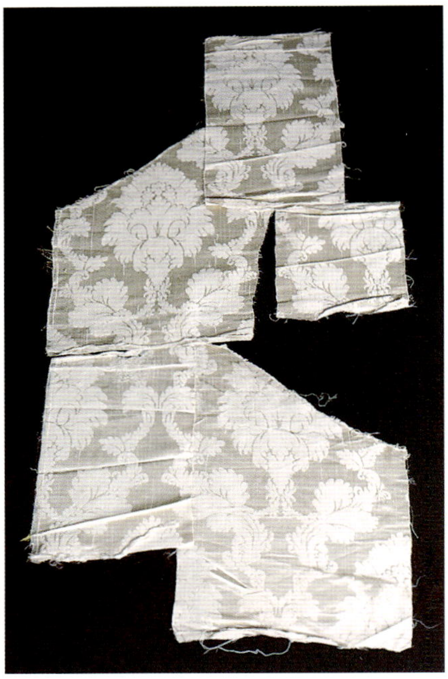

86 Dress silk
[RW23–28]
Late 17th century
Damask
17 × 15
(43 × 38);
P 18½ × 10¼
(47 × 26)
Remains of left selvedge on two pieces.

87 Woven silk and linen
[RW38]
Late 17th century
Damask
16¼ × 5½
(41.3 × 14);
P 7 (17.8) × ?
Probably from a striped pattern, rather than a border.

below
88 Woven silk
[RW543]
Late 17th century
Damask
24½ × 22¼
(62.3 × 56.5)
loom width;
P 30est. × 11¼
(76 × 28.5)

89 Border from a furnishing silk
[RW16]
Last quarter 17th century
Damask
28½ × 13½
(72.5 × 34.3)

left
91 Furnishing silk [RW17]
First half 18th century
Damask
23 × 21
(58.5 × 53.5)
loom width;
P ? × 20½ (52)

far left
90 Furnishing silk [RW11]
First half 18th century
Damask
23¼ × 25¼
(59 × 64) loom width;
P ? × 15 (38)

92 Furnishing or dress silk [RW18]
Early 18th century
Damask
19 × 25 (48 × 63.5) loom width; P ? × 25 (63.5)

93 Dress silk
[RW29]
Early 18th century
Damask
41 × 36½ (104 × 93) loom width 20.5 (52);
P 19¾ × 10 (50 × 26)
Mended with piece of 18th century painted silk.

94 Woven silk
[RW39]
Early 18th century
Damask
38½ × 11 (98 × 28);
P ? × 10½ (26.5)

95 Furnishing silk [RW40]
First half 18th century
Damask
34½ × 22 (87.5 × 55) loom width;
P ? × 10½ (26.5)
Re-dyed at later date, and lined with cotton.

96 Silk and linen furnishing [RW321–325]
Early 18th century
Damask
16 × 7½ (40.6 × 19)
Part of a valance with lower curved edge trimmed with a woven fringe of silver gilt filé.

97 Furnishing silk [RW448]
Early 18th century
Damask
39 × 41 (99 × 104.2) loom width 26½ (67.3); P 32½ × 26½ (82.5 × 67.4)

98 Dress silk [RW50]
c.1710
Three-coloured damask
17½ × 12½ (44.5 × 31.7); P 10 × 9½ (25.4 × 24.2)
Photographed from the back to show the pattern more clearly.

left
100 Dress silk [RW57]
1715 to 25
Two-coloured damask
43 × 21½ (109.2 × 52); P 14½ × 10¼ (36.8 × 26)

right
99 Furnishing silk [RW452]
Early 18th century
Damask
93 × 21½ (236.2 × 54.6) loom width; P 58 × 21 (147.5 × 53.4)

101 Woven silk [RW15]
1720s
Damask
19 × 21¾ (48 × 55) loom width; P ? × 9¼ (23.5)

102 Woven silk
[RW30]
1720s
Damask
25 × 6
(63.5 × 16.8);
P 14½ (36.8) × ?
Left selvedge.

103 Dress silk, 3 pieces
[RW51–53]
1720s
Two-coloured tabby damask
44½ × 21
(113 × 53.4)
loom width;
P 19¼ × 20½
(48.9 × 52)
Cut to make a cross orphrey for a chasuble.

104 Dress silk
[RW417]
c.1720
Two-coloured damask
39 × 39
(100 × 100);
P 17½ × 10
(44 × 25.5)

105 Dress silk
[RW453]
1720s
Two-coloured damask
40 × 21½
(101.6 × 54.6)
loom width;
P 14 × 20¾
(35.5 × 52.7)

right
106 Furnishing or dress silk
[RW12]
Second quarter 18th century
Damask
18½ × 20½
(47 × 52);
P ? × 9½ (24.2)

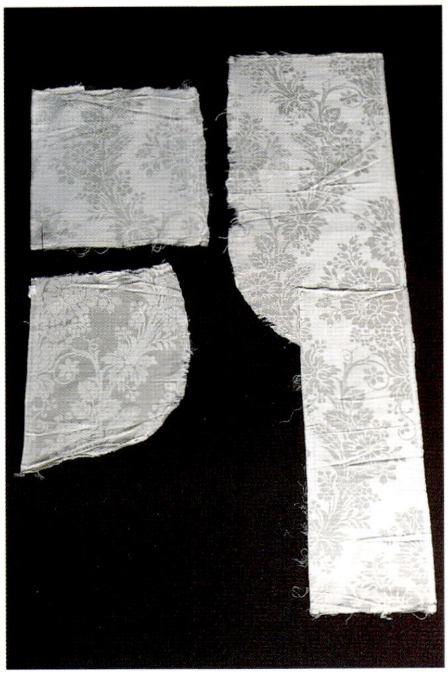

108 Furnishing or dress silk, probably ornament d'église
[RW19–22]
Second quarter 18th century
Damask
19½ × 9¾ (49.5 × 25); P 15¾ (40) × ?
Two pieces have selvedge.

above
107 Furnishing or dress silk, 4 joined pieces
[RW14]
Second quarter 18th century
Damask
23¼ × 20 (59 × 51); P 18¼ × 10 (46.5 × 25.5)

left
109 Furnishing or dress silk
[RW32]
Second quarter 18th century
Damask
43 × 9 (109 × 23); P 26½ (67) × ?
Re-used as a chasuble.

110 Silk furnishing
[RW423]
Second quarter 18th century
Damask
59 × 14 (150 × 35); P 49½ (126) × ?

111 Dress silk
[RW35]
Second quarter 18th century
Damask
45¼ × 10¾ (115 × 27.3); P 23¼ (59) × ?
One selvedge.

left
110 (lower part)

111 detail

112 Woven silk and linen
[RW41]
Mid 18th century
Damask
26½ × 20
(67.5 × 51) loom width 20 (51);
P 20¼ × 9½
(51.5 × 24)
Probably for upholstery.

113 Dress silk
[RW46]
1730s
Two-coloured damask
30 × 22
(76.2 × 56) loom width;
P 22¾ × 21½
(57.8 × 54.6)
Photographed from the back to show pattern more clearly.

114 Furnishing silk [RW449]
Mid 18th century
Damask
28 × 24¾
(71.1 × 63.5)
loom width;
P ? × 25 (63.5)

left
115 Furnishing silk [RW422]
1740s or 50s
Damask
25¼ × 22½
(64 × 57) loom width;
P ? × 21¾ (56)

below
116 Furnishing or dress silk, ornament d'église [RW31]
Second half 18th century
Damask
19 × 19 (48 × 48)
Possibly a chalice veil.

below
117 Dress silk
[RW62]
1750s
Two-coloured damask
14½ × 12½
(36.8 × 31.7);
P 8⅝ × 6⅜
(21.9 × 16.2)
Right selvedge.

118 Woven silk
[RW55 & 56]
Mid 1750s to early 1760s
Two-coloured damask
10 × 19½
(25.5 × 48.9);
P 11 × 19¼
(28 × 48.9)

119 Dress silk
[RW366]
1760s
Damask
20 × 12½
(52 × 32);
P 11 × 6¼
(28 × 16)
Overdyed at later time; originally white pattern on green.

120 Furnishing silk [RW533]
Late 18th century
Damask
101 × 111
(256.5 × 282);
P 47 × 20
(119.5 × 50.8)
Bedspread lined with woollen tabby cloth, with red cotton knotted fringe, which appears to be later in date.

below
121 Furnishing silk [RW5]
Late 19th century
Damask
18½ × 21¼
(47 × 54);
P 23½ × 10⅝
(58.5 × 26.7)
One selvedge.

122 Furnishing silk [RW34]
Second half 19th century
Damask
23 × 20¾
(58.5 × 52.5);
P 4¾ × 5¼
(12 × 13)

123 Silk furnishing
[RW347]
Second half 19th century
Damask
83 × 38
(120 × 96);
P 24 × 25½
(60 × 61)
The design, *Stambourne Basket*, was first used in the mid 18th century, and has continued to be popular ever since. Made up as a curtain, lined with red fine woollen cloth with machine-stitched seams.

124 Dress silk [RW348]
Second half 19th century
Damask
29¾ × 20 (74 × 50); P 19 × 10½ (47 × 26.7)
Hand sewn into panel with a brass ring at each top corner. Right selvedge.

125 Furnishing silk [RW349.1]
Second half 19th century
Damask
55½ × 64 (141 × 162.5); P 37½ × 27½ (95 × 70)
Based on silk designs of first half 18th century. One selvedge.

126 Woven silk and cotton [RW351]
Late 19th century
Damask
21 × 31 (53.4 × 79); P ? × 20 (50.8)
Right selvedge. Off settee from Moccas Court, Herefordshire, 1968

127 Silk furnishing [RW421]
Late 19th century
Damask
43 × 21½ (108 × 54.5); P ? × 29 est (73.7)

128 Furnishing silk [RW444]
Late 19th century
Damask
109 × 29½ (277 × 75); P 41 × 29½ (104 × 75)
A popular pattern for silks or wallpapers, it was hung at Hatfield, Kedleston, Stowe, Temple Newsam and elsewhere. Zoffany's current wallpaper *Small Villandry* is the same.

129 Woven silk [RW541]
1890s
Damask
43½ × 52 (110.5 × 132); P 11¼ × 6¾ (28.5 × 17)
An early 20th century reproduction of a 16th century Italian silk, by Warner & Sons.

130 Furnishing silk [RW445]
Early 20th century
Two-coloured damask
21½ × 28 (54.6 × 71.1); P 21½ × 21½ (54.6 × 54.6)
Sample length; pattern based on ornament designs c.1700.

131 Silk and linen furnishing [RW107]
Second half 16th century
Brocatelle weave
19¾ × 12 (50.2 × 30.5)

132 Silk and linen furnishing [RW108]
Second half 16th century
Brocatelle weave
24½ × 8⅛ (62.3 × 20.6); P 10¾ × 4½ (27.3 × 11.4)

133 Silk and linen furnishing [RW441]
Second half 16th century
Brocatelle weave
19¾ × 50 (50.2 × 127); P 15 × 11 (38 × 28)
Two half lengths joined selvedge to selvedge down the centre. Re-used as a chasuble.

134 Silk and linen furnishing [RW111]
First half 17th century
Brocatelle weave
38 × 29 (96.5 × 73.7); P ? × 21¼ (51.5)
Tape and cord, looped for suspension, attached along top edge on the back.

135 Silk and linen furnishing [RW109]
Second quarter 17th century
Brocatelle weave
25 × 8½ (63.5 × 21.6); P 17½ × 11est. (44.5 × 28est.)
Furnishing silk subsequently re-used to make a chasuble. Part of right selvedge remains.

136 Silk and linen furnishing
[RW106]
Third quarter 17th century
Brocatelle weave
23 × 8½ (58.5 × 21.6);
P 12½ × 7¾ (31.8 × 19.7)
Left selvedge.

137 Silk and linen furnishing
[RW112]
Probably late 17th century
Brocatelle weave
44 × 21 (111.7 × 53.4) loom width;
P ? × 20½ (52)
Provincial piece in a revised grotesque style.

138 Silk and linen furnishing [RW110]
Early 18th century
Brocatelle weave
15 × 7½ (38.2 × 19)

139 Silk and linen furnishing
[RW115]
First half 18th century
Brocatelle weave
41 × 25½ (104 × 64.7) loom width;
P ? × 25 (63.5)

140 Silk and linen furnishing
[RW118]
Early 18th century
Brocatelle weave
33 × 27¼ (83.8 × 69.3);
P ? × 26½ (67.3)
Five inch linen strip behind top portion, with looped suspension cord attached. The patttern is identical to that of RW119, Cat. no. 141 but woven to a larger scale.

141 Silk and linen furnishing [RW119]
Early 18th century
Brocatelle weave
15 × 24 (38.2 × 61) loom width
Nail holes where it was attached to wall.

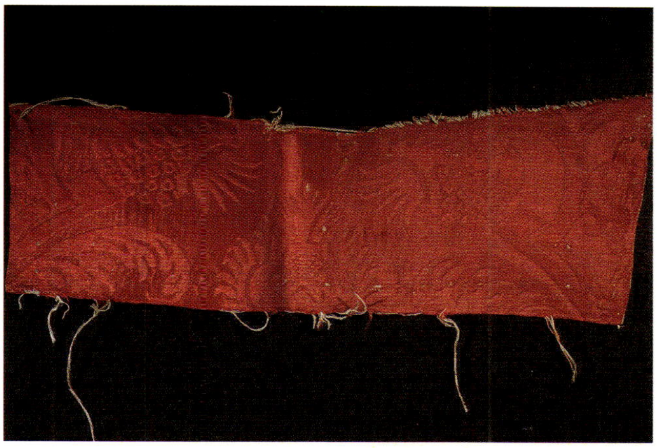

142 Silk and linen furnishing [RW120]
Early 18th century
Brocatelle weave
7½ × 20½ (19.5 × 52)

143 Woven silk and linen [RW542]
Early 18th century
Brocatelle weave
98½ × 49 (250 × 124.5); P 57 × 25 (145 × 63.5)
Ex Sam Wolsey, antique dealer, London, 1951 on closing down.

145 Silk and linen furnishing [RW410]
c.1700
Brocatelle weave
41 × 10½ (104 × 27); P 25 × 11est. (64 × 28est.)
Re-used as a chasuble, with part of yellow braid edging still in place.
Fragment of left selvedge.

144 Silk and linen furnishing [RW114]
Mid 18th century
Brocatelle weave
25 × 25 (63.5 × 63.5); P 29 × 24½ (73.7 × 62.3)
Tape and looped cord on back at top for suspension.

146 Silk and linen furnishing [RW326]
Mid 18th century
Brocatelle weave
8 × 16 (20.3 × 40.6)

147 Silk and linen furnishing [RW329]
Mid 18th century
Brocatelle weave
20 × 10½
(50.8 × 26.7)
Used to upholster the wing of a chair.

148 Silk and linen furnishing [RW330]
Mid 18th century
Brocatelle weave
10 × 20 (25.4 × 50.8); P ? × 22 (56) est.
Left selvedge.

149 Silk and linen furnishing [RW334]
Mid 18th century
Brocatelle weave
12 × 10½
(30.5 × 26.7)
One edge reinforced with coarse linen tape woven in pink and grey stripes.
One selvedge.

150 Silk and linen furnishing [RW335]
Mid 18th century
Brocatelle weave
18 × 13
(45.7 × 33) loom width c.22 (56);
P ? × 21½ (54.6)
One edge reinforced with coarse linen tape woven in pink and grey stripes.
Blue threads in selvedge.

151 Silk and linen furnishing [RW336]
Mid 18th century
Brocatelle weave
21¾ × 6½
(55.7 × 16.5)

152 Silk and linen furnishing [RW339]
Mid 18th century
Brocatelle weave
15½ × 20½ (39.4 × 52.1); P ? × 21 (53.3) est.
Right selvedge.

153 Silk and linen furnishing [RW317]
Second half 19th century
Brocatelle weave
13½ × 18 (34.3 × 45.7)
Cushion cover with piped edges and plain green cotton back. Machine stitched. The fabric imitates 18th century brocatelle in both pattern and technique.

154 Cotton and bast furnishing [RW337]
Late 19th century
Brocatelle weave
18¼ × 22½ (46.3 × 57.1); P ? × 12¾ (32.4)
Once a chair seat cover, with tack holes around the edge. Woven with a faintly streaky ground in imitation of a faded late 17th or 18th century silk.
Photographed from back to show pattern.

above & left (detail)
155 Dress or furnishing worsted [RW386–387.1]
Second quarter 18th century
Damask
41¼ × 6 (52 × 15) loom width 26¼ (66.7); P ? × 9½ (23)
12½ × 26¼ (31.8 × 68)
18½ × 14½ (47 × 36.8)

156 Worsted furnishing [RW490]
19th century
Damask
20 × 26 (50.8 × 66) loom width; P ? × 25 (63.5)

157 Worsted furnishing
[RW544.1]
19th century
Damask
69 × 75
(175.3 × 190.5)
loom width 26;
P 31¾ × 24⅜
(80.2 × 61.9)

158 Worsted furnishing
[RW385]
19th century
Damask
38½ × 25
(98 × 62) loom width 25¾ (66);
P 27½ × 25¼
(70 × 65.5)
Hand-sewn, with silk geometric patterned ribbon down one side.

159 Worsted furnishing [RW491]
19th century
Damask
25 × 50 (63.5 × 127) loom width 26 (66);
P 30 × 25½ (76 × 25.5)
Hem edged with yellow patterned tape.

160 Worsted furnishing
[RW492]
19th century
Damask
30 × 51
(76.2 × 129.5)
loom width;
P 12 × 10
(30.5 × 25.5)
Lined with fine woollen twill.

161 Worsted furnishing
[RW493]
19th century
Damask
90 × 25½
(228.6 × 64.8)
loom width;
P 40 × 25
(101.6 × 63.5)

162 Worsted furnishing [RW494]
19th century
Damask
36 × 48 (91.5 × 122) loom width 26 (66);
P 20¾ × 26 (52.7 × 66)
Has been a curtain, gathered at the top, with purple and yellow woven tape along two edges.

163 Worsted furnishing
[RW496]
19th century
Damask
31 × 19
(78.8 × 48.2);
P 27½ × c.25
(70 × 63.5)
Typical mid 18th century pattern, but reduced in scale.

164 Worsted furnishing [RW371]
Mid 19th century
Damask
21 × 65 (52 × 192) loom width c.25½ (65)
Bed valance pleated onto tube of plain worsted; hem trimmed with red woollen twill tape. Both selvedges.

165 Worsted furnishing
[RW374]
Mid 19th century
Damask
97 × 50
(244 × 127);
P 11½ × 10
(30 × 26)
Curtain, roughly hand-sewn; the top 17in. folded over and metal eyes sewn through the fold.

166 Worsted furnishing [RW375]
Mid 19th century
Damask
75 × 50 (188 × 127) loom width; P 5¾ × 4 (15 × 10.5)

167 Worsted furnishing
[RW377]
Mid 19th century
Damask
82 × 46½
(208.3 × 118.1)
loom width 49.5
(125.7);
P 10 × 8
(25 × 20.5)
Curtain, hand-sewn and edged on three sides with pink and cream silk ribbon with key pattern.

168 Worsted furnishing [RW122]
Second half 19th century
Damask
67½ × 24½ (171.5 × 62.3) loom width; P 30 × 24 (76.2 × 61)
Contemporary blue wool trim down right hand side.

169 Worsted furnishing [RW340]
Third quarter 19th century
Damask
18¼ × 23¾ (45 × 57); P 10½ (26.5) × ?
Chair seat cover with tack holes and some tacks.

170 Worsted furnishing [RW373]
Second half 19th century
Damask
67 × 36 (164 × 93) loom width 25 (63.5); P 26 × 25 (66 × 64)
Hand-sewn as curtain edged with purple silk ribbon with a geometric pattern.

171 Worsted furnishing [RW376]
Third quarter 19th century
Damask
76 × 47½ (193 × 122) loom width 49 (124.5); P 13¼ × 8¼ (33.5 × 21)
Curtain edged on three sides with pink and cream ribbon with serpentine pattern.

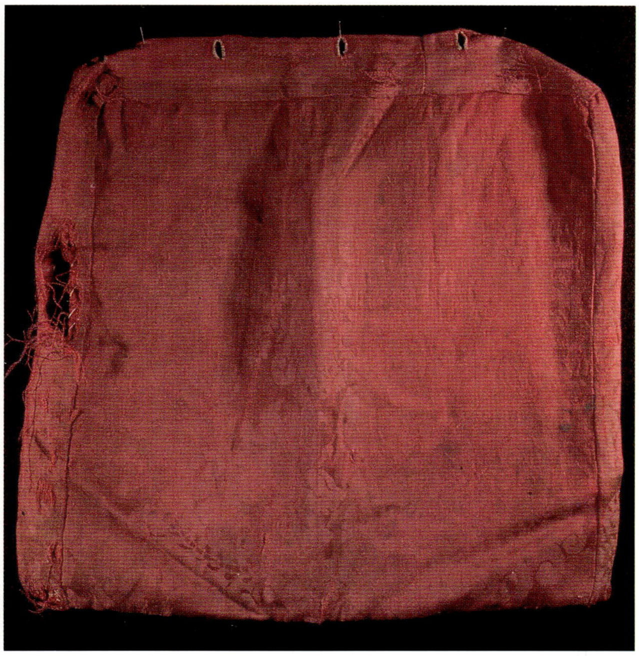

left
173 Worsted furnishing [RW379]
Third quarter 19th century
Damask
67 × 66 (167 × 166) loom width 47½ (120.7); P 7 × 4 (17 × 10)

left
172 Worsted furnishing [RW378]
Second half 19th century
Damask
17½ × 18½ × 2¼ (44.5 × 46 × 5.5); P ? × 18 (45.7) est.
Cushion cover hand-sewn with buttons made from self-covered brass rings, finished with woollen tape.

174 Worsted furnishing [RW384]
Second half 19th century
Damask
93 × 52 (236.2 × 132)
loom width 26¼ (66.7);
P 31¼ × 26 (80 × 66)
Made up as a swag, from two widths hand-sewn together, with the pattern running horizontally.

175 Worsted furnishing [RW415]
Second half 19th century
Damask
23 × 27 (60 × 70)
cushion cover.

176 Wool and bast furnishing [RW338]
Late 19th century
Damask
23¼ × 36 (57 × 90); P 15¾ × 10⅝ (40 × 27)
Ex S. W. Wolsey Ltd. Right selvedge.

left
175 detail

177 Worsted furnishing [RW383]
Late 19th century
Damask
58 × 46 (145 × 120) loom width 49 (124.5);
P 14¾ × 10 (37 × 25)
Curtain, edged down each side with gold-coloured cotton and silk brocaded tape with fleur-de-lis motif. Drawstring cotton tape along top edge.

178 Worsted furnishing [RW443]
Late 19th century
Two-coloured damask
13 × 25 (33 × 63.5); P 8 × 6½ (20.3 × 16.5)

179 Worsted furnishing
[RW495]
Late 19th century
Complex weave
27 × 22
(68.6 × 56);
P ? × 8¾ (22.2)

180 Worsted furnishing
[RW380]
Last quarter 19th century
Damask
47½ × 22½
(118 × 57);
P 9½ × 8¼
(24 × 21)
Curtain with tape along top edge, and ribbon trim along left edge.

181 Woven wool and linen [RW121]
Date uncertain
Twill weave
11 × 25½ (28 × 64.8)

182 Wool shawl
[RW437]
1820s
Complex weave
56 × 56
(142.2 × 142.2);
P 5½ × 3½
(14 × 9)

183 Wool and linen furnishing [RW453.1]
Late 18th or early 19th century
Hand knotted
45 × 54 (114.3 × 137.1); P 21½ × 6½ (54.5 × 16.5)
Part of a carpet, possibly made at Wilton, heavily abraded and mended by hand. Bought at Wilton House sale, 25 May 1960, inside cupboard, lot 27.

184 Wool and cotton furnishing [RW125]
Late 19th century
Complex weave, double cloth
33½ × 55 (85 × 139.7); P 20½ × 11½ (52 × 29.2)
Machine-woven to give the effect of tapestry. RW126 is a cover of the same fabric (see checklist).

186 Wool and cotton furnishing [RW389]
c.1900
Complex weave
16½ × 21¼ (42 × 54)
Right selvedge.

above
185 Wool furnishing [RW128]
Late 19th century
Complex weave, cut-pile
13½ × 13 (34.3 × 33)
Carpet border, probably from Kidderminster or Glasgow.

left
188 Linen furnishing [RW267.1]
Early 20th century
Damask
239 × 137 (607 × 348); P 14½ × 15¼ (37 × 38.5)
Drugget, for protecting carpets.

187 Linen furnishing [RW420.1]
Early 20th century
Damask
66 × 49 (167.5 × 124.5); P 9½ × 4½ (23.5 × 11.5)
By Arthur Lee, sample piece.

189 Wool furnishing [RW532]
Probably first half 20th century
Twill weave
90 × 71 (228.6 × 180.3); P 9 × 7½ (23 × 19)
Blanket, originally from Cheviot area. Ex Vincent Kelly, antique dealer, Whitehaven, Cumbria.

opposite

190 Wool furnishing [RW369]
Probably first half 20th century
Twill weave
80 × 73 (203 × 185.5)
Blanket, originally from Cheviot area. Ex Vincent Kelly, antique dealer, Whitehaven, Cumbria.

191 Wool furnishing [RW370]
Probably first half 20th century
Twill weave
82 × 72½ (208 × 184)
Blanket, originally from Cheviot area. Ex Vincent Kelly, antique dealer, Whitehaven, Cumbria.

192 Woven linen and silk [RW392]
Possibly 15th century, German
Complex weave
17½ × 4 (44 × 10);
P 1½ (3.5) × ?
Cf. Agnes Geijer, *A History of Textile Art* (Pasold/Sotheby, 1979), fig. 82, e,f.

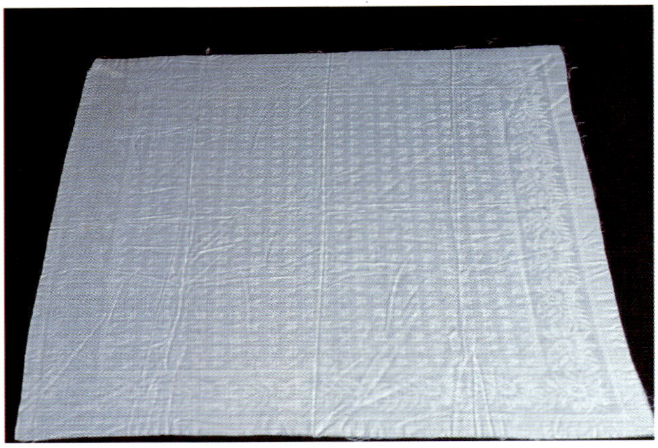

193 Woven linen [RW523]
19th century
Complex weave
20½ × 20 (52 × 50.8)
Probably intended for a handkerchief, but not yet hemmed.

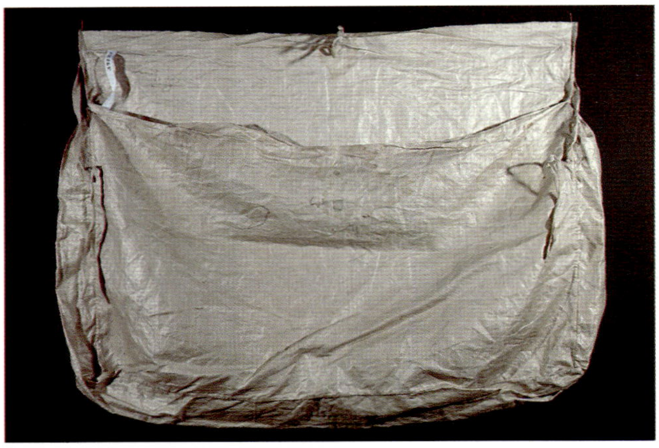

194 Linen furnishing [RW265]
18th or 19th century
Tabby weave
15 × 26 × 3½ (38.1 × 66 × 8.9)
Under slip-cover for a pillow, with a flap opening along the long edge, fastened with three pairs of cotton twill tapes. Calandered to make it feather-proof.

195 Linen furnishing [RW258]
Second half 18th century
Tabby weave
25 × 24 (60 × 59); P 2 × 2 (5 × 5)
Hemmed and seamed by hand, and edged with light blue and white tape woven in chequered pattern.

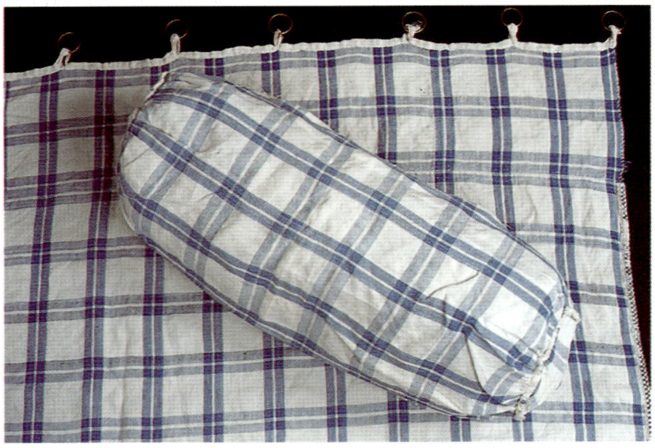

196 Linen furnishing [RW263 & 263.1]
Second half 18th century
Tabby weave
22 × 5½ (56 × 14); P 3 × 2¾ (7.6 × 7) bolster cover
39 × 48 (99 × 121.9); P 3 × 2¾ (7.6 × 7) curtain, cut-down
Also matching sofa squab.

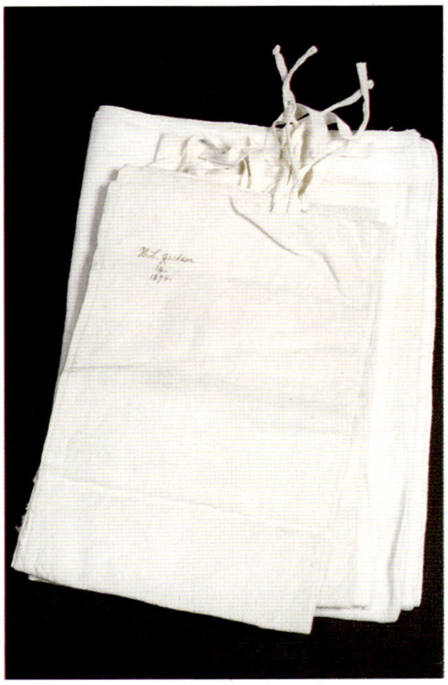

197 Linen furnishings [RW525–527]
1871, 1874
Tabby weave
17½ × 26½ (44.5 × 67.3)
Three pillowcases with simple opening with no overlap and two pairs of tapes to fasten. Inscribed in black ink in top left corner
E. Jackson./40./187;
H.L. Jackson./4./1874

198 Silk and linen furnishing [RW132]
Late 18th century
Tabby weave
13 × 51 (33 × 129.5); P ? × 10½ (26.7)
Valance, lined with coarse linen, bound with yellow silk with a coarse linen tape stitched along back of top edge, from which the valance was suspended.

199 Cotton furnishing [RW133]
Late 18th century or early 19th century
Complex weave
74 × 61½ (188 × 156.2); P ground stripes 4–6 (10–15) apart
Known as a Caddow Quilt, commonly made in Bolton, Lancashire. The design is typical, although the striped ground is rare.

200 Cotton furnishing [RW256]
19th century
Tabby weave
24½ × 18¾ (60 × 47); P 2 × 2 (5 × 5)

201 Furnishing cotton [RW257]
19th century
Tabby weave
43¼ × 11 (110 × 28); P 4 × 4 (10 × 10)

202 Cotton furnishing [RW264]
Early 20th century
Twill weave
to fit a 54 × 78 mattress (200 × 300); P 3¾ × 4 (9.5 × 10)
Part of a hand-stitched mattress cover with marks of the buttoning which held the stuffing in place.

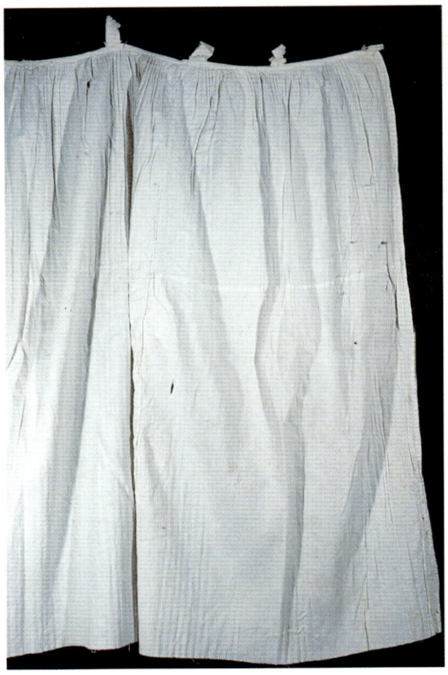

203 Cotton furnishing [RW408]
Early 19th century
Complex weave
91 × 61½
(231 × 156)
Bed furniture of dimity, including two long finely gathered curtains stitched onto tape with loops, and two short curtains with loops.

204 Cotton shawl [RW436]
Mid 19th century
Jacquard weave
45 × 90
(114.3 × 228.6);
P 3½ × 1
(8.9 × 2.5)

205 Cotton furnishing [RW127]
c.1900
Complex weave
87 × 8 (221 × 20.3); P 10½ (26.7) × ?
Frieze or border with fringe trim made from wefts tied in bunches.

206 Cotton furnishing [RW419]
20th century
Damask
24½ × 51
(60 × 140);
P 22½ × 13
(58 × 32.5)
Mid 18th century design, scaled down and repeated four times in the width.

207 Furnishing worsted [RW489]
c.1700
Ribbed tabby weave, stamped
10½ × 38 (26.7 × 96.5) loom width 26 (66); P ? × 26 (66)

208 Furnishing worsted [38.1/85]
1740s
Ribbed tabby weave, stamped
28 × 16
(71.1 × 45.2)
Chair back.

209 Furnishing linen [RW407]
Probably 18th century
Ribbed tabby weave, stamped
32 × 5½ (82 × 14)
Photographed from back to show pattern more clearly.

210 Worsted furnishing [RW394]
Second half 19th century
Ribbed tabby weave, stamped
29 × 26½ (77 × 62); P 22½ (57) × loom width?
Possibly sofa seat cushion cover.

211 Worsted furnishing [RW399]
Probably 19th century
Ribbed tabby weave, watered
16½ × 25 (43 × 74)

212 Worsted furnishing [RW285]
Second quarter 19th century
Ribbed tabby weave, watered
16 × 90 (40.6 × 228.6) loom width 22⅞ (58)
Valance or pelmet of two layers of fabric bound with twill wool tape, trimmed with thick woollen fringe, and looped braid.

213 Woven silk [RW404]
Possibly 18th century
Tabby weave, watered
17¾ × 20½ (45 × 52)

214 Wool furnishing [RW123]
Mid 19th century
Cut pile velvet, stamped
10¼ × 24¼ (26 × 61.6) loom width; P ? × 24 (61)

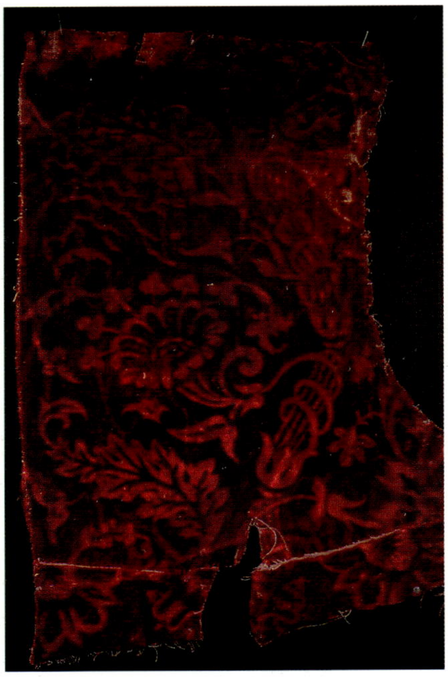

215 Worsted furnishing [RW314]
Second half 19th century
Cut pile velvet, stamped
15¾ × 20 (40 × 51)
Nail holes and one nail, and evidence of hand stitching.

216 Worsted furnishing [RW572]
Mid 19th century
Cut pile velvet, stamped
23 × 9½ (58.5 × 24.2); P 11¾ × ? (29.9 × ?)

218 Furnishing or dress silk [RW438]
Probably 19th century, Turkish
Cut pile velvet on metal ground lamé with silver gilt strip
19 × 33 (48.2 × 83.9); P 3 × 2 (7.5 × 5)
Lining of purple cotton with green bias cotton edging.

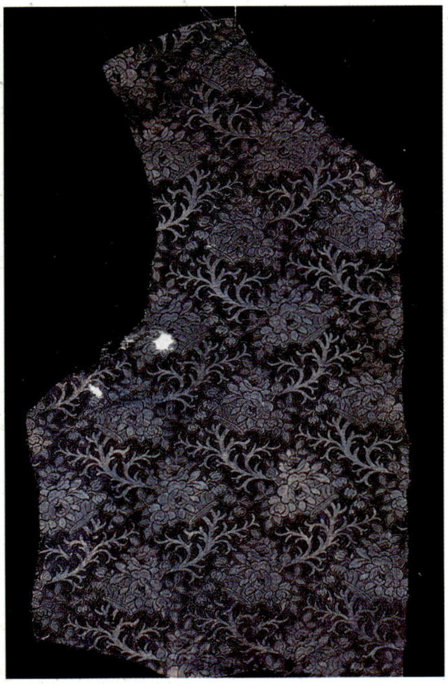

above
217 Worsted furnishing [RW573]
Mid 19th century
Cut velvet pile, stamped
8½ × 9½ (21.6 × 24.2)

left
219 Dress silk [RW357]
Second half 19th century, Oriental
Complex weave
15½ × 9 (39 × 23); P 4 × 2¾ (10 × 7.5)
Originally cream and blue, overdyed at a later date.

220 Woven silk [RW72]
Late 19th century, Japanese
Complex weave with Japanese gold pattern wefts
23½ × 17½ (59.7 × 44.5); P 32 × 7 (81.3 × 17.8)

Printed

Previous page:
Printed cotton, detail of Cat. no. 270 [RW135]

left
221 Printed cotton [RW146]
Possibly 17th century
Block-printed
40½ × 14½ (102.8 × 36.8); P 23 (58.5) × ?
A problem piece, this could be a late 19th century pastiche.

222 Pencilled cotton [RW136]
Second quarter 18th century, Indian
Pencilled
28 × 36½ (71 × 92.7); P c.23 × c.17½ (58.5 × 44.5)
Ex Horace Warner, bought by him and Reginald in Low Countries early 20th century.

below
223 Pencilled cotton sleeves [RW478]
Late 18th century, Indian
Pencilled
7 × 4 (17.8 × 10.2)
Pair of child's sleeves with embroidered detail and buttons; lined with plain cotton, with ties at top to attach to bodice. Ex Horace Warner, bought by him and Reginald Warner in Low Countries, early 20th century.

224 Pencilled cotton [RW477]
Late 18th century, Indian
Pencilled
36 × 18 (91.5 × 45.7); P c.2 (5) × ?
Ex Horace Warner, bought by him and Reginald Warner in Low Countries, early 20th century.

225 Pencilled cotton [RW478.1]
c.1750, Indian
Pencilled
36 × 62 (91.5 × 157.5); P ? × c.29 (73.7)
Skirt border, bought by Horace Warner c.1900, possibly in Dordrecht, Low Countries, whilst travelling with Reginald Warner.

227 Pencilled cotton [RW481]
Late 18th century, Indian
Pencilled
14 × 21 (31.7 × 53.3); P 16 × 16 (40.6 × 40.6)
Ex Horace Warner, bought by him and Reginald Warner in Low Countries, early 20th century.

226 Pencilled cotton [RW480]
Late 18th century, Indian
Pencilled
12½ × 14 (31.7 × 35.5); P ? × c.10 (25.4)
Ex Horace Warner, bought by him and Reginald Warner in Low Countries, early 20th century.

228 Pencilled cotton [RW479]
Late 18th century, Indian
Pencilled
13 × 25 (33 × 63.5); P ? × 21 (53.4)
Ex Horace Warner, bought by him and Reginald Warner in Low Countries, early 20th century.

229 Pencilled cotton [RW482]
Late 18th century, Indian
Pencilled
19 × 26½ (48.2 × 67.3); P c.16¼ × c.20½ (41.3 × 52)
Ex Horace Warner, bought by him and Reginald Warner in Low Countries, early 20th century.

230 Pencilled cotton [RW483]
Late 18th century, Indian
Pencilled
27½ × 17 (70 × 43.2); P c.8 × c.10 (20.3 × 25.4)
Probably drawn from a European-style pattern layout, but motifs are Indian. Ex Horace Warner, bought by him and Reginald Warner in Low Countries, early 20th century.

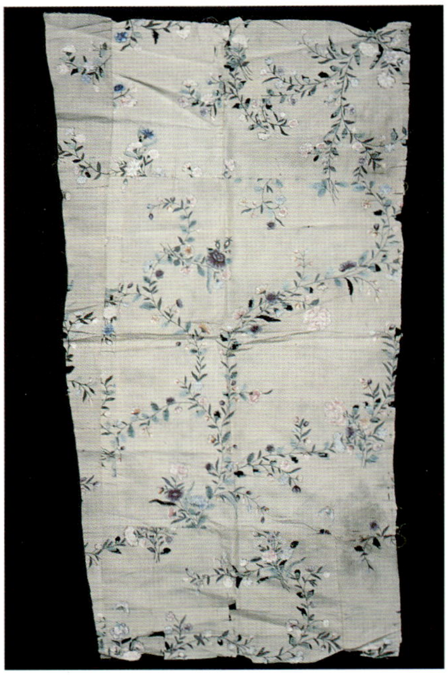

231 Pencilled silk [RW552]
Late 18th century
Pencilled
40½ × 21½ (102.9 × 54.7)

232 Printed cotton furnishing [RW530]
c.1780
Block-printed
80 × 58 (203.2 × 147.3); P 12 × 19 (30.5 × 48.2)
Quilted coverlet, red cotton lining later than rest. Probably from Mulhouse, France, in the *Indienne* style.

233 Printed cotton [RW467]
Last quarter 18th century
Block-printed and pencilled
73 × 5 (185.5 × 12.7); P 11 × 4¼ (28 × 10.3)

234 Printed cotton furnishing [RW195]
Last quarter 18th century
Block-printed
16 × 74 (40.6 × 188) loom width 28 (71.1);
P ⅞ × 1¾ (2.3 × 4.5)
Made up as a bed valance, with tapes on the top and left edges.

235 Printed cotton, 13 joined pieces [RW141]
Early 19th century, probably French
Roller-printed
34 × 16
(86.4 × 40.7)

236 Printed cotton [RW147]
c.1783 (design)
Copper-plate printed
54 × 35 (137.2 × 88.9); P 37est. × 73½ (94 × 186.7)
A later print of a 1783 copper-plate design, *Hommage de l'Amerique à la France*. Original printed in red at Jouy, France. (Example in Musée Oberkampf.)

237 Printed cotton, 5 joined pieces [RW142]
Early 19th century, probably French
Copper-plate printed
37½ × 7
(95.3 × 17.8)

238 Printed cotton furnishing [RW145]
c.1792, French
Copper-plate printed
15 × 48 (38 × 122)

Quilted valance, design *le Char de l'Aurore*, plate-printed in red by T.P. Meillier & Cie. of Beautiran near Bordeaux, 1792. Scene from Ovid's *Metamorphoses*, after le Guide. (Piece showing complete pattern at the H.F. du Pont Winterthur Museum, Wilmington, Delaware (58.35.7).)

239 Printed cotton furnishing [RW139]
c.1811, French
Roller-printed
46 × 37 (117 × 94) from top of chair back to front seat rail; P 18 (45.8) × ?
Chair cover with inscriptions in French. Fastened with tapes and press studs.

240 Printed cotton furnishing [RW140]
1821, French
Copper-plate printed
15 × 69 (38 × 175.3)
Valance printed with scenes from the life of Belisaire, with inscriptions in French. Signed in the print *Caron Sculpt. 1821*

241 Printed cotton [RW144]
c.1825
Copper-plate printed
$42 \times 6\frac{1}{4}$ (106.7×16); P $18\frac{1}{4}$ (46.4) × ?

242 Printed cotton huswife [RW547]
Late 18th or early 19th century
Block-printed
$12 \times 2\frac{3}{4}$ (30.5×7); P $4\frac{1}{4}$ (10.8) × ?

243 Printed cotton reticule [RW574]
Early 19th century
Block-printed
$9\frac{3}{4} \times 8\frac{1}{4}$ (24.8×21); P ? × 6 (? × 15.3)

below
245 Printed cotton [RW211]
Early 19th century
Block and roller-printed
$17 \times 16\frac{1}{2}$ (43.2×41.9); P $13\frac{1}{2}$ (34.3) × ?

244 Printed cotton [RW211.1]
Early 19th century
Block and roller-printed
14×26 (35.6×66) loom width; P $12\frac{1}{2}$ (31.8) × ?

246 Printed cotton [RW426]
Early 19th century
Block and roller-printed
38 × 124 (96.5 × 316) loom width ?; P ½ × ¼ (1.3 × 1.3)

247 Printed cotton [RW466]
c.1804
Block-printed
7 × 14½ (17.8 × 36.8); P 3¼ × 2½ (8.3 × 6.3)
Probably printed for E. Dudding

248 Printed cotton [RW165]
First quarter 19th century
Block-printed
6½ × 10½ (16.5 × 26.7); P 1⅛ × ¾ (2.8 × 1.9)

249 Printed cotton [RW465]
c.1804
Block-printed
45 × 7 (114.3 × 17.8); P 39 (99) × ?
Probably printed for E. Dudding. A very similar design was printed by Bannister Hall, 1805.

250 Printed cotton [RW148]
c.1805
Block-printed
9 × 20 (23 × 50.8); P 6¾ × 9 (17.2 × 22.9)
Designed by J.J. Pearman for Richard Ovey & Co., Covent Garden, printed by Bannister Hall. A Chinoiserie border was also printed with it. (S.McA. ref. C/462.b.)

251 Printed cotton furnishing [RW208]
1814 to 16
Block-printed
52 × 25 (132 × 63.5); P 16 × 26est. (40.7 × 66)
Bannister Hall (S.McA. ref. C/4848). A popular design of the period, this was originally a cover or curtain.

252 Printed cotton [RW183]
1815 to 30
Block-printed
10¾ × 11¾ (27.3 × 29.9); P 5 × 1⅝ (12.7 × 4.2)

right
253 Printed cotton [RW468]
1815 to 30
Block-printed
17½ × 11½ × 21 (44.5 × 29.2 × 53.3); P 2¼ × 1¾ (5.7 × 4.5)
Doll's bed furniture; loops are brought from inside and hooked over buttons to fasten back curtains.

254 Printed cotton [RW172]
First half 19th century
Roller-printed
16 × 9 (40.7 × 22.9)
RW172 and 173 are examples of Hoyle's purple, the best fast purple dye of this period. This style of print is what was known as calico in America. Compare Cat. no.290 [RW151].

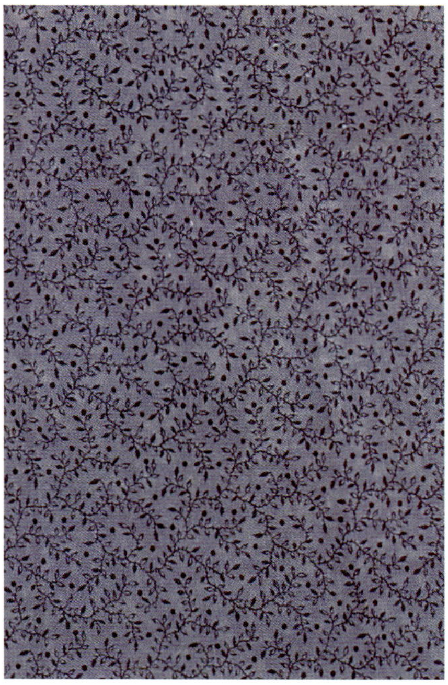

255 Printed cotton [RW173]
First half 19th century
Roller-printed
15½ × 11 (39.4 × 27.9); P 1½ × 2¾ (3.8 × 7)

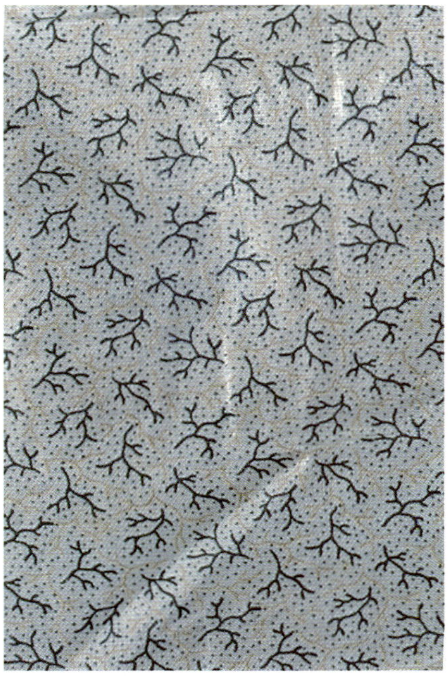

256 Printed cotton [RW167]
1820s onwards
Roller-printed
5¾ × 23¾
(14.6 × 60.3);
P 1¼ × 2½
(3.2 × 6.4)

left
257 Printed cotton [RW212]
1820s, based on late 18th century style
Block and roller-printed
70 × 8
(177.8 × 20.4);
P 13¾ (35) × ?

258 Printed cotton [RW213]
1820s
Roller-printed
18 × 23 (45.7 × 58.4) loom width; P 12¼ × 17 (31.1 × 43.2)

below
259 Printed cotton [RW214]
1820s
Roller-printed, starch glazed
12¾ × 13½
(32.4 × 34.3)

260 Printed cotton furnishing
[RW215]
1820s
Roller-printed
68 × 49
(172.8 × 124.5), two loom widths;
P 13½ × 12¼
(34.3 × 31.1)
Curtain, bound with tape in blue and brown with brass curtain rings attached with tape loops.

261 Printed cotton [RW217]
1820s
Block-printed
57½ × 49
(146 × 124) loom width 33 (83.7);
P 16¼ × 13¼
(41.3 × 33.7)

262 Printed cotton [RW218]
1820s
Block-printed
21 × 7¼
(53.3 × 18.4);
P 11½ (29.2) × ?

263 Printed cotton [RW219]
1820s
Block and roller-printed
11 × 8 (28 × 20.3)

264 Printed cotton [RW229]
1820s
Roller-printed
54 × 24¾
(62.9 × 37.2); P
14¾ (37.5) ×
loom width but
repeat does not
match
Pattern of 1820s,
but colour might
indicate 1880s or
90s print.

265 Printed cotton furnishing
[RW469]
1820s
Roller-printed
36 × 11¼
(91.5 × 28.5);
P 17½ (44.5) × ?
Lined with plain
cotton and bound
along three sides
with cotton tape.

266 Printed cotton [RW186]
19th century
Roller-printed on
dimity weave
4¼ × 17¾
(10.8 × 45.1); P
⅝ × ½ (1.6 × 1.3)

267 Printed cotton [RW190]
19th century
Roller-printed on dimity weave
6 × 12 (15.2 × 30.5); P 1⅛ × ½ (2.8 × 1.8)

268 Printed cotton [RW185]
19th century
Roller-printed
5½ × 4
(14 × 10.2);
P 1⅛ × 2¼
(2.9 × 5.7)
Similar example with a leafy infill in Stead McAlpin archive.

269 Printed cotton [RW170]
Second quarter 19th century
Block and roller-printed
22½ × 31½
(57.2 × 80) loom width;
P 2⅛ × 1⅝
(5.4 × 4.1)

270 Printed cotton [RW135]
Second quarter 19th century
Block-printed and pencilled
24½ × 83 (62 × 211)
Probably Italian, part of a mezzara, consisting of lower border and bottom right corner.

271 Printed cotton [RW155–157]
Second quarter 19th century
Block-printed
13½ × 6¼ (34.3 × 15.9); P 2½ × 2⅛ (6.4 × 5.4)

272 Printed cotton [RW158–160]
Second quarter 19th century
Block-printed
10 × 6 (25.4 × 15.3); P 3⅛ × 6⅜ (7.9 × 16.2)

273 Printed cotton [RW200]
1825 to 30
Block and roller-printed
28 × 18 (71 × 45.7); P 15½ × 17 (39.4 × 43.2)
Attributed to Stead McAlpin c.1810–20 in W. Gordon Hunton, *English Decorative Textiles*, 1930.

274 Printed cotton [RW476]
c.1825
Block-printed
16 × 27 (40.6 × 68.6); P 13¼ × 23 (33.6 × 58.4)

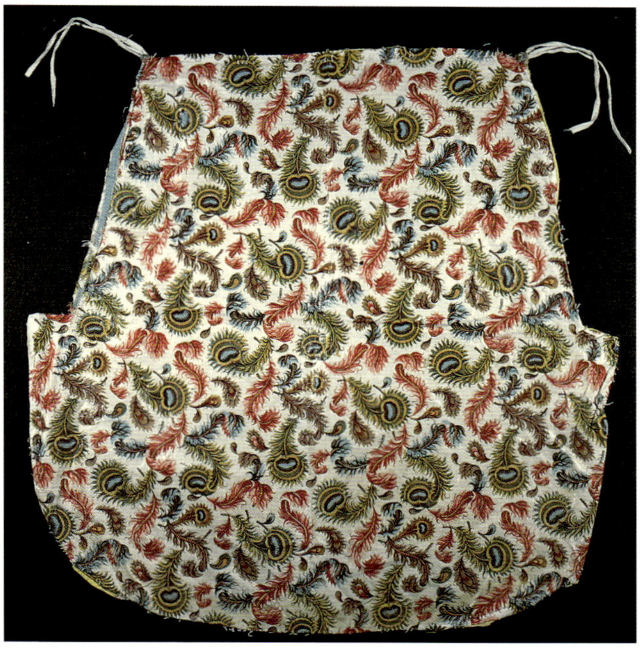

276 Printed cotton furnishing [RW198]
1829
Block-printed
25 × 43 (63.5 × 109.2); P 12½ × 9 (31.8 × 22.9)
Bannister Hall, for Clarkson and Turner. Machine stitched curtain (S.McA. ref. C/6405).

above
275 Printed cotton furnishing [RW222]
1826
Block-printed, glazed
22 × 22½ (55.8 × 57.2);
P 10½ × 8¼ (26.7 × 21)
Bannister Hall, seat cover with tapes at two back corners lined with bright yellow cotton; design last printed 1943 (S.McA. ref. C/6219).

left
277 Printed cotton [RW149]
c.1830
Block-printed
27½ × 19¾ (70 × 50.2);
P ⅞ × 1½ (2.2 × 3.8)
Several similar designs in Stead McAlpin archive.

above **273** detail *below* **280** detail

278 Printed cotton [RW161]
1830s
Block-printed, glazed
11 × 8
(28 × 20.4);
P 7 × 4¾
(17.8 × 12.1)

279 Printed cotton [RW164]
1830s
Block-printed
6 × 12
(15.3 × 30.5);
P ¾ × 1⅜
(1.9 × 3.5)

280 Printed cotton [RW163]
1849, roller-printed
29 × 24 (73.7 × 61): P 9½ × 8½ (24.2 × 21.6)
Printed by Bannister Hall for Miles and Edwards (S.McA. ref. K/2719). Design taken from a ceiling at Crewe Hall, Cheshire, published by C.J. Richardson, *Studies from Old English Mansions*, Second Series, June 1842.

281 Printed cotton furnishing [RW475]
c.1837
Roller-printed
30 × 15½
(76.2 × 39.4);
P 3½ × 2¼
(8.9 × 5.7)
Made up into a rectangular cushion case, with a plain piece of cotton for the underside. Stead McAlpin for Miles and Edward (S.McA. ref. K/2036).

282 Printed cotton [RW199]
c.1830s
Block-printed
16¾ × 19¾ (42.6 × 50.2); P 16 × 19 (40.7 × 48.3)
Based on late 18th century-style pattern, and could even be printed from blocks of that period.

283 Printed silk stole [RW488]
1860s
Block-printed
102 × 24
(259 × 61) loom width;
P 12¼ × 24
(31.1 × 61)

above **282** detail *below* **286** detail

284 Printed cotton furnishing [RW471]
c.1830s
Block-printed
12½ × 24 (31.7 × 61); P 16 × 16 (40.6 × 40.6)
Valance, lined with olive green cotton and edged with green woollen braid, with loops of tape stitched to the top edge.

285 Printed cotton furnishing [RW197]
1835 to 45
Block and roller-printed
16 ¾ × 28½ (42.5 × 72.3); P 12¾ × 25est. (32.4 × 63.5)
Valance, lined with cotton and edged with a striped tape.

286 Printed cotton [RW228]
1830s to 50s
Roller-printed
13 × 27 (33 × 68.6) loom width; P 14 × approx. 26 (35.6 × 66)

287 Printed cotton [RW203]
1835 to 50
Block and roller-printed
27 × 18¾ (68.6 × 47.6); P 13¼ (33.7) × ?

288 Printed cotton [RW209]
1835 to 50
Block and roller-printed
19 × 15 (48.3 × 38); P 12 × 18½ (30.5 × 47)

289 Printed cotton [RW232]
First half 19th century
Block-printed with roller-printed ground
50 × 13 (127 × 33) loom width 25 (63.5); P 14¼ × 22½ (36.2 × 57.2)
Design in style of 1830s, but could be a later print from rollers of that date.

290 Printed cotton [RW151]
c.1837
Block-printed, with roller-printed ground
17 × 13 (43.2 × 33); P 9¼ × 8½ (23.5 × 21.6)
Stead McAlpin (S.McA. ref. K/1802).

291 Printed cotton [RW162]
c.1837
Block-printed with roller-printed ground
27½ × 31½ (69.9 × 80) loom width 26¼ (66.6); P 5⅜ × 7¼ (13.7 × 18.4)
Stead McAlpin for Thos. Clarkson & Co. (S.McA. ref. K/1574).

292 Printed cotton furnishing [RW216]
1840
Block-printed
24½ × 32 (62.2 × 81.3); P 17¼ × 16½ (43.8 × 41.9)
Stead McAlpin for Albert & Crocker, London. Lined with cotton printed with arabesque design in beige. RW220, Cat. no. 293, includes the border to this pattern.

293 Printed cotton furnishing [RW220]
1840
Block-printed
16½ × 36½ (42 × 92.7); P as RW216, Cat no. 292, with border 16½ (42) × ?
Bed valance, lined with cotton roller-printed with arabesque pattern. Hand sewn, pleated onto tube, edged with silk woven tape (S.McA. ref. K/2336).

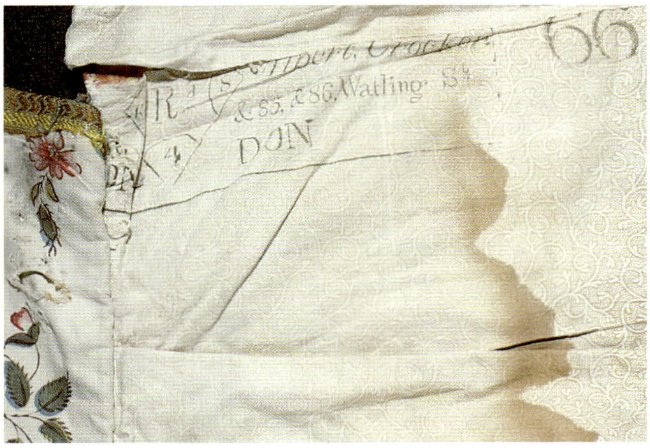

294 Printed cotton furnishing [RW220.1]
1840s
Roller-printed
16½ × 36½ (42 × 92.7)
Lining to RW220. Has company stamp of Albert & Crocker/... and 85, and 86, Watling St/... London, and design registration stamp current 1842–1867.

295 Printed cotton furnishing [RW485]
1840s
Block and roller-printed
13½ × 33½ (34.3 × 85.1); P 9 × 8½ (22.8 × 21.6)
Valance bound with red twill cotton tape.

296 Printed cotton [RW485.1]
1840s
Roller-printed
13½ × 33½ (34.3 × 85.1); P 5 × (12.7 × 5)
Lining to RW485.

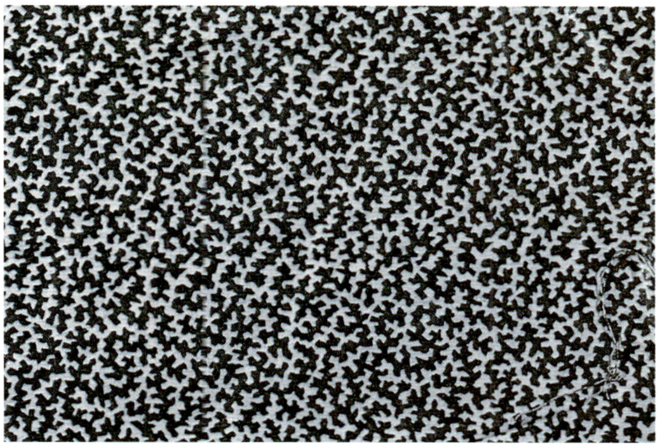

297 Printed cotton [RW154]
c.1837
Block-printed
8½ × 6 (21.6 × 15.3); P 2⅞ × 2½ (7.3 × 6.4)
Very similar to Stead McAlpin (S.McA. ref. K/1557).

left
298 Printed cotton [RW150]
Mid 19th century
Roller-printed
14 × 15 (35.6 × 38.1); P 1⅛ × 8¼ (2.8 × 21)

right
299 Printed cotton furnishing [RW531]
c.1848
Block-printed
94 × 94 (239 × 239)
Coverlet, inscribed 1848 on the reverse.
Bought by RW in Bourton-on-the-Water, 1980.

300 Printed cotton [RW169]
Mid 19th century
Block-printed, calendered
14 × 24½ (35.6 × 62.2) loom width; P 1½ × 1 (3.8 × 2.6)

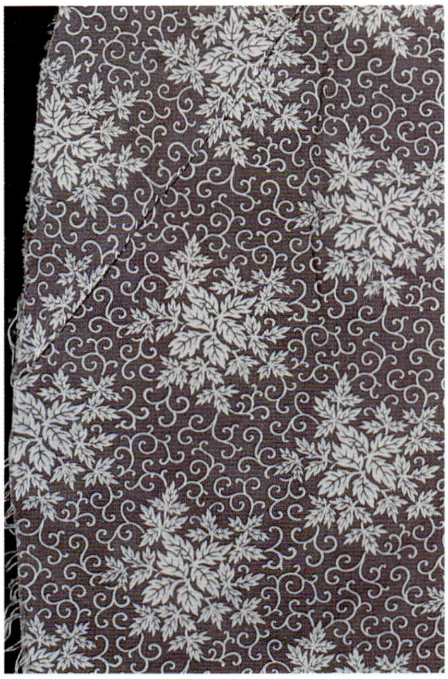

301 Printed cotton [RW171]
Mid 19th century
Roller-printed
9 × 31½
(22.9 × 80);
P 4¾ × 2½
(12.1 × 6.4)

302 Printed cotton [RW181]
Mid 19th century
Roller-printed
14 × 11½ (35.6 × 29.2); P 4⅝ × 11¼ (11.8 × 28.6)

303 Printed cotton [RW201]
Mid 19th century
Block and roller-printed
8½ × 21½ (21.6 × 54.6); P ? × 12½ (31.8)

304 Printed cotton [RW221]
Mid 19th century
Roller-printed
20 × 25½ (50.7 × 64.7) loom width; P 13 × 12¼ (33 × 31.1)

305 Printed cotton [RW134]
Mid 19th century, possibly Persian
Block-printed
68 × 49½ (173 × 125.7)
Two pieces sewn together before printing.

left
306 Printed cotton [RW223]
1850
Block-printed
14½ × 17 (36.8 × 43.2); P 12½ × 5 (31.7 × 12.7)
Stead McAlpin for Miles and Edward (S.McA. ref. K/2728).

right
307 Printed cotton [RW204]
1860s, possibly French
Block-printed with roller-printed ground
47½ × 12 (120.7 × 30.5); P 15½ (39.4) × ?

below left
308 Printed cotton [RW227]
1851
Block-printed
128 × 9½ (325 × 24.2); P 17½ (44.5) × ?
Bannister Hall, for Swainston and Dennys (S.McA ref C/8025). Cf. RW196, Cat. no. 310.

above
309 Printed cotton [RW153]
1860s
Roller-printed
15 × 18⅛ (38 × 46); P 4¾ × 8¼ (12.1 × 21)

310 Printed cotton [RW196]
1860s
Block and roller-printed, calandered
15 × 21 (38 × 53.4); P 7½ × 7¼ (19.1 × 18.4)

311 Printed cotton [RW225]
1864
Block-printed with roller-printed ground
80 × 15 (203.2 × 38); P 19¾ × 17 (50.2 × 43.2); lining 2 × 1½ (5.1 × 3.8)
Stead McAlpin. (S.McA. ref. K/4131), originally as filling with border. Blocks destroyed 1964. This has the extra roller-printed ground.

left
312 Printed cotton furnishing [RW425]
c.1860s
Roller-printed
35 × 24 (85 × 60); P 26 × 29 (66 × 74)
Window or bed furniture of heavy cotton rep. Lined with beige rep, edged with heavy woollen tasselled fringe.

right
313 Printed cotton furnishing [RW230]
1865
Block-printed
35 × 35½ (89 × 90.2)
Seat cover, hand sewn, lined with cream cotton. Stead McAlpin. (S.McA. ref. K/4713).

314 Printed cotton furnishing [RW174.1]
1866
Block-printed, calandered
38½ × 48¼ (97.8 × 122.6); P 24 × 32½ (61 × 81.3)
Magnolia, Bannister Hall (S.McA. ref. C/9270). Curtain made up of 4 separate squares, lined with pale blue cotton with tape and ties along top edge and ribbon edging on two sides.

315 Printed cotton [RW231]
c.1870
Block-printed
29 × 32 (73.7 × 81.3); P 15¾ × 26¾ (40 × 67.9)
Bannister Hall. Originally printed as filling with border, also printed later by Ramm and Crocker, last printed 1959 (S.McA. ref. C/9405).

317 Printed cotton [RW174]
Third quarter 19th century
Block and roller-printed
21 × 16½ (53.3 × 41.9); P 13 (33) × 28 (71.1)

316 Printed cotton [RW472]
Late 1860s to 70s
Block and roller-printed
10½ × 58 (26.7 × 147.3); P 22½ (57.2) × ?

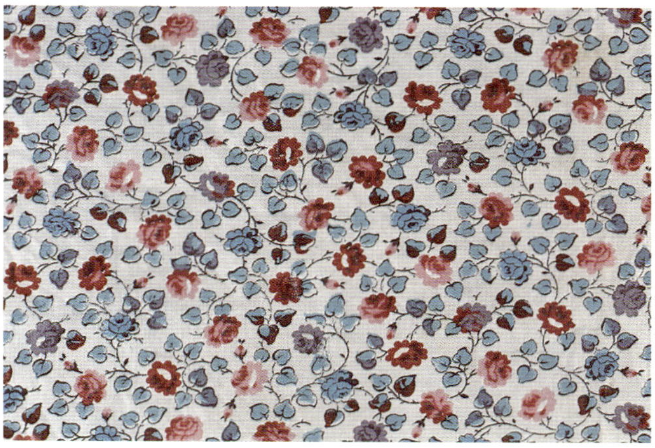

318 Printed cotton [RW179]
Third quarter 19th century
Mule-printed
11 × 30 (28 × 76.2); P 4¼ × 8¾ (10.8 × 22.2)
Machine-hemmed in chain-lock stitch with draw-string along long edge.

319 Printed cotton [RW474]
Third quarter 19th century
Block and roller-printed
47 × 20 (119.4 × 50.8); P 3 × 1¾ (7.6 × 4.5)

320 Printed cotton [RW193]
1860s to 70s
Block-printed
24 × 8½ (61 × 21.6); P 5 × 5⅛ (12.7 × 13)
Same material as RW194, Cat. no. 321

321 Printed cotton furnishing [RW194]
1860s to 70s
Roller-printed
14½ × 16 (36.8 × 40.7); P 5 × 5⅛ (12.7 × 13)
Tie-back for curtain lined with green cotton in a darker shade, edged with woollen woven looped braid in green and red.

323 Printed cotton [RW207]
1873
Block and roller-printed
22½ × 23 (57.2 × 58.5); P 7 (17.8) × ?
Stead McAlpin. (S.McA. ref. K/5257)

322 Printed cotton [RW168]
1871
Block and roller-printed
19½ × 25 (49.5 × 63.5) loom width; P 2 × 2⅛ (5.1 × 5.4)
Stead McAlpin. (S.McA. ref. K/5054)

324 Printed cotton [RW553]
Second half 19th century
Roller-printed
106 × 31 (269.3 × 78.8) loom width;
P 7 × 11½ (17.8 × 29.2)

325 Printed cotton [RW187]
Second half 19th century
Roller-printed on dimity weave
19¾ × 9¼ (50.2 × 23.5); P 3¼ × 3⅜ (8.2 × 8.6)

326 Printed cotton [RW189]
Second half 19th century
Roller-printed on dimity weave
13 × 8½ (33 × 21.6); P 1 × ⅞ (2.6 × 2.2)

327 Printed cotton [RW191]
Late 19th century
Roller-printed
7 × 8½ (17 8 × 21.5); P 2¼ × 2¼ (5.7 × 5.7)

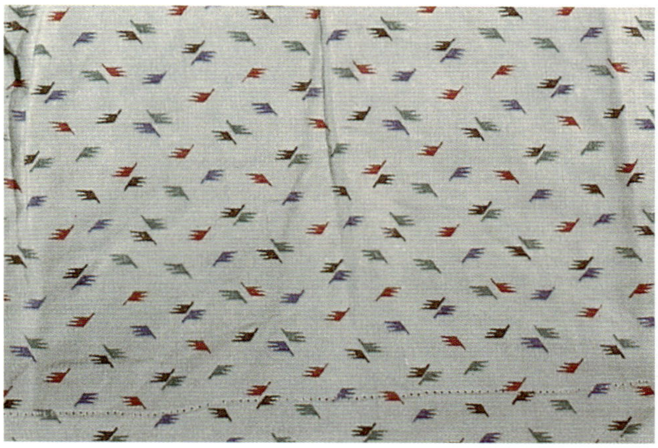

328 Printed cotton [RW182]
Late 19th century
Roller-printed
5 × 9¾ (12.7 × 24.8); P 3 × 3¾ (7.7 × 9.5)

329 Printed cotton furnishing [RW226]
Second half 19th century
Roller-printed
21 × 33 (53.3 × 78.8); P ? × 33 (78.8) loom width
Cushion cover.

330 Printed cotton [RW470]
Late 19th century
Roller-printed
11½ × 11½
(29.2 × 29.2)

332 Printed baize [RW486]
Second half 19th century
Block-printed
29 × 13 (73.7 × 33); P 24¾ (62.9) × ?

331 Printed baize [RW388]
1868
Block-printed
70 × 70 (180 × 180) loom width; P 11⅝ × 12¼ (29.5 × 31)
RW's attached label says *stated to have been purchased 1868 at Harrods by Martha Jarvis of Windrush, Glos. year of her marriage to serg. David Hamilton of the Scots Guards. Per Mrs Alice Williams, Willow Cottage, Little Barrington, Glos.*

333 Printed cotton furnishing [RW238]
1875
Block-printed
9 × 68½ (22.9 × 174); P 21½ × 9 (54.5 × 23)
Tulip designed by William Morris. Lined with cream wool with blue dotted scroll design edged with fancy braid. Selvedge marked [MORRIS & COMPA]NY.26 QUEEN SQR BLOOMSBUR[Y].

334 Printed cotton [RW239]
c.1876
Block-printed
40½ × 28 (101.6 × 71.2); P 11½ × 9 (29.2 × 23)
Snakeshead designed by William Morris.

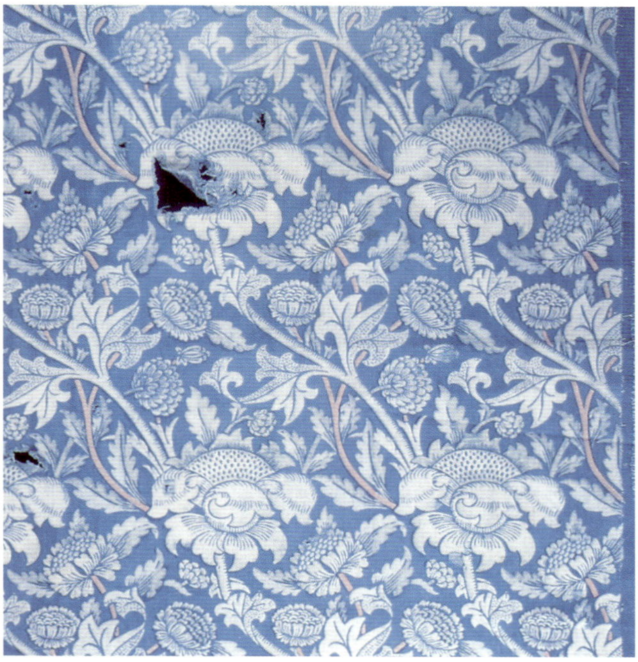

335 Printed cotton [RW487]
c.1883
Block-printed
26 × 29 (66 × 73.7); P 9 × 12 (30.5 × 22.8)
Wey designed by William Morris. Selvedge marked REG^{D} MORRIS & COMPANY 449 OXFORD STREET LONDON W – the most commonly used mark for the period 1877–1917.

336 Printed cotton [RW246]
c.1883
Block-printed
9 × 10 (23 × 25.5); P 9 × 12 (23.5 × 30.5)
Wey designed by William Morris. Selvedge marked REG^{D} MORRIS & COMPANY 449 OXFORD STREET LO[NDON].

337 Printed cotton [RW237]
1882
Block-printed
13½ × 5½
(34.3 × 14);
P ?
Brer Rabbit designed by William Morris.

338 Printed cotton [RW249]
1883
Block-printed
84 × 50
(213.5 × 127);
P 19¾ × 18¼
(50.2 × 46.4)
Rose designed by William Morris.
Badly faded.

339 Printed cotton [RW251]
1883
Block-printed
13 × 14 (33 × 35.5); P 4⅜ × 4¼ (11.1 × 10.8)
Flowerpot designed by William Morris.

340 Printed cotton furnishing [RW248]
1885
Block-printed
16½ × 30 (42 × 76.2); P 17 × 12 (43.2 × 30.5)
Medway designed by William Morris. Curtain made with pattern running horizontally, with tracking hand sewn along top edge.

341 Printed cotton furnishing [RW240]
Late 19th century
Roller-printed
34½ × 25 (87.5 × 63.5); P 15 × 9½ (38.2 × 24.2)
A flat slipcover with press stud fasteners at the corners. Design in the style of William Morris.

above left
342 Printed cotton furnishing [RW241]
Late 19th century
Block-printed
43 × 40 (109 × 101.6); P 14½ × 32 (36.8 × 81.3)
Curtain, design in the style of William Morris.

above right
343 Painted canvas [RW254]
Late 19th century
Painted
24 × 20 (61 × 50.7); P 20¾ × 20¾ (52.7 × 52.7)
Late 17th century-style design for a repeating pattern.

344 Printed cotton [RW175]
1880s
Roller-printed
8½ × 4¼ (21.6 × 10.8); P 2⅜ (6) × ?

345 Printed cotton [RW177]
1880s
Block-printed with roller-printed ground
17 × 15 (43.2 × 38.1); P 5¼ × 5¾ (13.4 × 14.6)

346 Printed cotton [RW178]
1880s
Block-printed on twill
4 × 7¼ (10.2 × 18.4); P 3⅞ × 3½ (9.8 × 8.9)

347 Printed cotton [RW180]
1880s
Roller-printed on twill
5½ × 4¾
(14 × 12.1)

348 Printed cotton [RW176]
1880s to 90s
Roller-printed
7 × 13½ (17.8 × 34.3); P 2¼ × 4¾ (5.7 × 12.1)

left
349 Printed cotton [RW184]
1880s to 90s
Roller-printed
11½ × 4
(29.2 × 10.2);
P 1¾ × 1½
(4.5 × 3.8)

right
350 Printed cotton [RW484]
1887
Roller-printed
37 × 30
(94 × 76.2);
P 2¾ × 3½
(7 × 8.9)
Made for Queen Victoria's Jubilee, 1887.

left
351 Printed cotton [RW188]
Late 19th century
Roller-printed
7 × 2½
(17.8 × 6.4);
P 2⅛ × 3
(5.4 × 7.7)

right
352 Printed cotton [RW192]
Last quarter 19th century
Roller-printed
3 × 8¾
(7.6 × 22.2);
P ? × 2½ (6.4)

354 Printed cotton [RW244]
1898
Block-printed, discharge
49 × 41 (124.5 × 104), loom width 32½ (82.5);
P 13¼ × 15¾ (33.7 × 40)
The New Dot designed by Lewis F. Day.

355 Printed linen and cotton [RW252]
Early 20th century
Block-printed
23 × 30½ (58.5 × 77.5); P 17 × 14 (43.2 × 35.6)

353 Printed silk
[RW255]
1890s
Screen-printed
33 × 28 (84 × 71);
P ? × 23½ (59.5)
Probably design for a border, in the style of C.F.A. Voysey; very badly registered.

357 Printed cotton [RW166]
Early 20th century
Block-printed with roller-printed ground
24½ × 30¼ (62.2 × 76.8); P 15½ × 14¾ (39.9 × 37.5); ground 1⅛ × 1⅛ (2.8 × 2.8)

356 Printed cotton [RW234]
1898
Roller-printed
51 × 29½ (129.5 × 75); P 17¼ (43.8) × probably loom width, half drop
Stead McAlpin for Stonards (S.McA. ref. K/8235).

358 Printed cotton [RW205]
Early 20th century
Roller-printed
26 × 15 (66 × 38.1); P 19¾ (50.2) × ?
20th century version (possibly screen-printed) of 19th century design.

359 Printed cotton furnishing [RW202]
20th century
Roller-printed
h.24½ × w.28 (62.2 × 70.1); P 14½ × 10 (37 × 25.5)
Loose cover for upholstered easy chair.

360 Printed cotton [RW206]
Early 20th century
Roller-printed
38 × 31 (96.5 × 78.8) loom width; P 16 × 10 (40.6 × 25.4)
Two pieces both with rusty nail holes and marks where hooks were attached, indicating the fabric was used to line a wardrobe.

361 Printed cotton furnishing [RW233]
Early 20th century
Roller-printed
47 × 28 × 13½ (119.4 × 71 × 34.3); P 18 × 31½ (45.8 × 80) loom width
A settee seat cover, with gathered valance round three sides, and one straight side of plain cotton.

362 Printed linen [RW253]
20th century
Screen-printed
32 × 38½ (81.3 × 97.8); P 13½ × 12 (34.3 × 30.5)
A very good reproduction, probably hand screen-printed in imitation of block-printing, with a design of the 1830s.

363 Printed cotton [RW137]
c.1915 to 30
Roller-printed
17½ × 37 (44.5 × 94)
Revival of late 18th century style, probably using experimental technique of spray-gun colouring.

364 Printed cotton [RW224]
1910s
Block-printed
44½ × 50 (113 × 127); P 17¾ × 25 (45 × 63.5)

365 Printed cotton [RW138]
Late 19th century?
Block-printed
89 × 13¾ (226 × 34.8) loom width; P 7¼ × 13¾ (18.5 × 34.8)
Possibly Oriental obi (sash) width – used in the near and far east.

Embroidered

366 Wool and silk on linen [RW507]
Second half 16th century
Cross stitch
24 × 22½ (60.5 × 57.2); P ? × 14½ (36.8)
Part of cushion cover, with two near-contemporary borders added.

below
368 Linen on linen [RW535]
c.1600
Chain, satin and raised overcast stitches with cut-work and needle-made fillings
36 × 20 (91.5 × 50.8)
Pillowcase (detail), probably from the greater Cotswold area, where it was acquired.

367 Woven linen, silk and metal strip on silk [RW320]
17th century
Small motifs backed with paper and edged with couched linen thread
13½ × 39½ (33.5 × 100)
Made up as a valance.

369 Worsted on fustian [RW276]
1650s
Stem, link, long-and-short, speckling, and back stitches
29½ × 39⅜ (75 × 100) loom width 15 (38);
P 18 × 11 (28 × 21)
Part of a furnishing, possibly a table-cover.

Opposite page:
Wool on linen, detail of Cat. no. 371 [RW279]

above
370 Wool on linen [17/85]
Late 17th century
Knotted
21½ × 22¾ (54.5 × 58)
Back panel of backstool.

illustrated page 84
371 Wool on linen [RW279]
c.1700
Irish stitch. 48 × 77 (122 × 196; P 12¾ × 8¾ (32.5 × 22)
This type of embroidery was popular from the 16th century well into the 18th century, by which time woven copies were being made.

372 Worsted on fustian
[RW129]
Late 17th or early 18th century
Long-and-short, stem, encroaching satin, fish-bone, bullion and buttonhole stitches
28 × 17½
(71 × 44.5)
One side of a workbag for holding crewel wools.

373 Worsted on fustian [RW130]
Early 18th century
Long-and-short and stem stitches, with French knots, the lattice ground in backstitch
20 × 23 (50.7 × 58.4)
Part of a set of bed-hangings. Ex collection Commander Hart, Chipping Camden, Gloucestershire.

374 Worsted on fustian [RW274]
Late 17th century
Encroaching satin, stem, coral and speckling stitches
4 × 26 (10.2 × 66); P ? × 10 (25.4)
Fragment of border from a set of bed-hangings.

375 Worsted on fustian
[RW271]
Early 18th century
Coral, herringbone and encroaching satin stitches
14 × 12
(35.5 × 30.5)
Fragment of bed furniture from Cusworth Hall, Doncaster.

376 Worsted on fustian [RW278]
Early 18th century
Satin, stem, chain, and laid-and-couched stitches, with French knots
13 × 18½ (53 × 47)
Unfaded and probably never used.

377 Silk and linen [RW273]
Early 18th century
Back, satin, buttonhole, and herringbone stitches
17 × 12½ (45 × 31)
From Moccas Court, Herefordshire, 1947.

378 Linen on linen [RW498]
First quarter 18th century
Two layers with trapunto quilting
7½ × 20 (19 × 50.8);
P ? × 8 1/4 (21)
Part of coverlet.

379 Linen on linen [RW500]
Second quarter 18th century
Back-stitch
18 × 19 (45.7 × 48.3);
P 7 × 6½ (17.8 × 16.5)

380 Silk on linen [RW499]
First quarter 18th century
Back stitch
10 × 17 (25.5 × 43 2); P 5 1/4 × 10½ (13.3 × 26.6)

382 Worsted on linen [RW508]
Early 18th century
Chain and some satin stitch, quilted in running stitch
48 × 30 (122 × 76.2)
Made up into a small cover, possibly from a petticoat.

left
381 Silk on linen [RW433]
Early 18th century
Chain, buttonhole and satin stitches
24½ × 30 (62 × 76); P 13½ × 19½ (33 × 49)
From bed-furnishings, the design influenced by Indian chain-stitch embroidery.

383 Silk on wool [RW549]
Early 18th century
chain stitch or tambour work
8 × 4.25 (20.3 × 10.8); P ? × ?
Meandering floral sprays in polychrome. Sewn to letter from Fotheringay Castle. (Shown with RW550, linen with chain stitch in silk).

384 linen embroidered with silk [RW551]
Early 18th century
Chain stitch or tambour work, and French knots
10 × 6.5 (25.4 × 16.5)
From a garment. Probably from Moccas Court, Herefordshire.

above and left
385 Silk on cotton [RW504]
1720s to 30s, Indian
Hooked needle, or *ari*, work
19 × 22½ (48.2 × 57.2)
Made for Western market, the vermicular ground added.

386 Silk on silk [RW277]
1720s
Long-and-short, and satin stitches, with bullion and French knots and couched lines of twisted thread; backed with unspun wool and woollen cloth, quilted together in running stitch
21 × 21½ (53.4 × 54.6)

387 Silk on cotton [RW269]
Second quarter 18th century
Back, buttonhole, chain and satin stitches
18 × 23.5 (46 × 60); P 11 × 12.5 (28 × 31.7)
A bedcover re-used as a seat cover; the motifs influenced by Chinese and Indian embroidery.

388 Wool on fustian [RW412]
Second quarter 18th century
Chain stitch
21 × 29 (54 × 75)

389 Worsted on fustian
[RW513]
Second quarter 18th century
Chain stitch
40 × 50 (101.6 × 127) loom width 17½ (44.5); P ? × 28 (71.1)
Originally a petticoat.

390 Worsted on fustian [RW534]
Second quarter 18th century
Stem, buttonhole, laid-and-couched work and French knots
61½ × 20 (153.7 × 50.8) loom width
Laid out with robings and edging for a gown, never used.

391 Silk on silk [RW512]
1730s to 40s
Long-and-short, stem and satin stitches
16 × 41 (40.6 × 104.2)
Decorative apron edged with silver bobbin lace.

392 Linen on fustian [RW501]
1740s
Satin, padded overcast, and buttonhole stitches, with French knots and pulled fabric fillings
29 × 12 (73.7 × 30.5)
Waistcoat front.

393 Silk on linen [RW503]
second quarter 18th century
Stem, long-and-short, and laid-and-couched stitches, with French knots and speckling
28 × 15.5 (71.1 × 39.4)
Probably from bed furniture.

above
394 Wool on linen canvas
[RW536]
1740s to 50s
Cross and tent stitches
7 1⁄4 × 24
(18.4 × 61)
From a chair or sofa back.

left
395 Silk huswife
[RW502]
Late 18th or early 19th century, probably Indian export
Metal purl, tinfoil, glass beads, mirror glass, and painted silk on silk, trimmed with silver bobbin lace and narrow braid of silk and silver strip.
16 × 5½
(40.6 × 14)

396 Wool on wool [38.1/85]
1740s
Roumanian, open herringbone and stem stitches
26 × 23 (66 × 58.5)
Back panel of backstool.

397 Wool on linen [63⁄87]
1760s
Cross stitch
21 × 27 (53.3 × 68.5)
Seat panel of chair.

398 Silk on cotton [RW510]
c.1776
Chain, satin, stem, long-and-short stitches
42 × 22 (106.7 × 55.9); P 23½ × 11½ (59.7 × 29.2)
Part of a dress; similar patterns appeared in the *Lady's Magazine* during the 1770s.

399 Cotton on cotton [RW517]
c.1800–1810
Running stitch
36 × 72 (91.5 × 183); P 5 × 3 1⁄4 (12.7 × 8.2)
From a muslin gown.

400 Cotton on cotton [RW519]
Late 18th century, Probably Indian for western market
Tambour or *ari* work
33 × 48 (83.9 × 122); P 7 × 5.5 (17.8 × 14)

402 Silk and metal thread on linen [RW539]
19th century, Northern Turkish Bokhara
couching, stem and herringbone stitches
23¾ × 7¾ (60.3 × 19.7); P 11¾ (29.2) × ?

403 Silk on cotton [RW540]
19th century, Greek
Cretan feather, stem and whipped stem stitch
18 1⁄4 × 8 (46.4 × 20.3); P ? × ?
Probably from a garment.

401 Paint on canvas [RW515]
19th century
Shaded for the guidance of the embroiderer
28½ × 21½ (72.4 × 54.6)
Unused needle-work design for seat back and arms.

above
404 Silk on wool [RW516]
Second quarter 19th century, possibly Russian
Satin, stem, long-and-short, and straight stitches
28 × 20¾ (71.1 × 52.7)
The end of a stole.

left
405 Silk on silk gauze [RW414]
19th century, Chinese
counted satin stitch
14 × 13.5 (35 × 35)
Lined with blue silk and bound with black. Put together from pieces of a robe. Inscribed in oriental script on reverse with symbols meaning Spring, Peace, Safety, Birth, and in lattice junctions, Longevity.

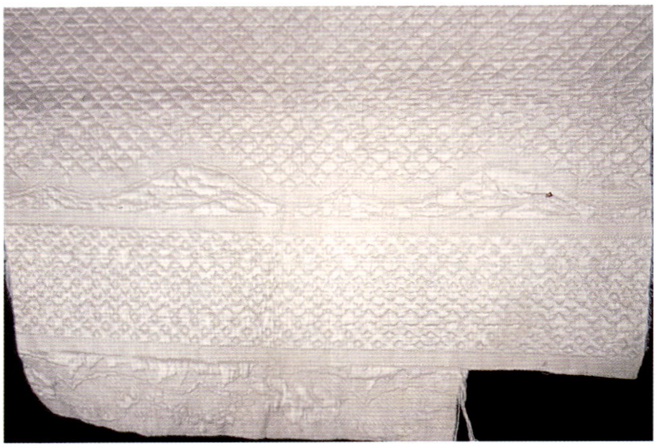

406 Silk on silk [RW509]
1840s to 50s
tabby weave with quilting
32 × 17 (81.3 × 43.2)
Machine-woven to look like hand quilting. Probably from a layette.

408 Silk on silk [RW411]
Late 19th century, Turkish for the European market
Chain stitch and French knots
46½ × 17 (120 × 40)
Made up as a cushion.

410 Silk on linen [RW497]
Early 20th century
Running and other straight stitches
5 × 9 (12.7 × 22.8)
Meant for the yoke of a child's dress.

407 Silk on silk patchwork
[RW270]
c.1860s–90s
Applied soutache braid
21 × 19.5
(53.3 × 49.5)
The templates, cut from old letters, remain behind the diamonds.

409 Metal threads on silk velvet [RW297]
c.1900, Indian for western market
Split spangles, round and square purl, gilt wrapped on a thick silk core, and gilded copper ornaments; couched work
32 × 42 (81.3 × 106.7)
Possibly the front panel of formal gown.

above
411 Linen napkin
[RW520]
c.1630
Damask
42 × 28½
(106.7 × 72.4)
Embroidered PEM 1630.
Ex widow of Albert Warner, eldest son of Metford Warner.

left
412 Linen tablecloth
[RW522]
c.1630
Damask
108½ × 83
(275.6 × 210.8);
P 47 × 23¾
(119.5 × 60.3)
Large tablecloth depicting Abraham and Isaac. ? Dated 1626. Ex Mrs Andrew Mein, Dutton Lodge, Cheshire.

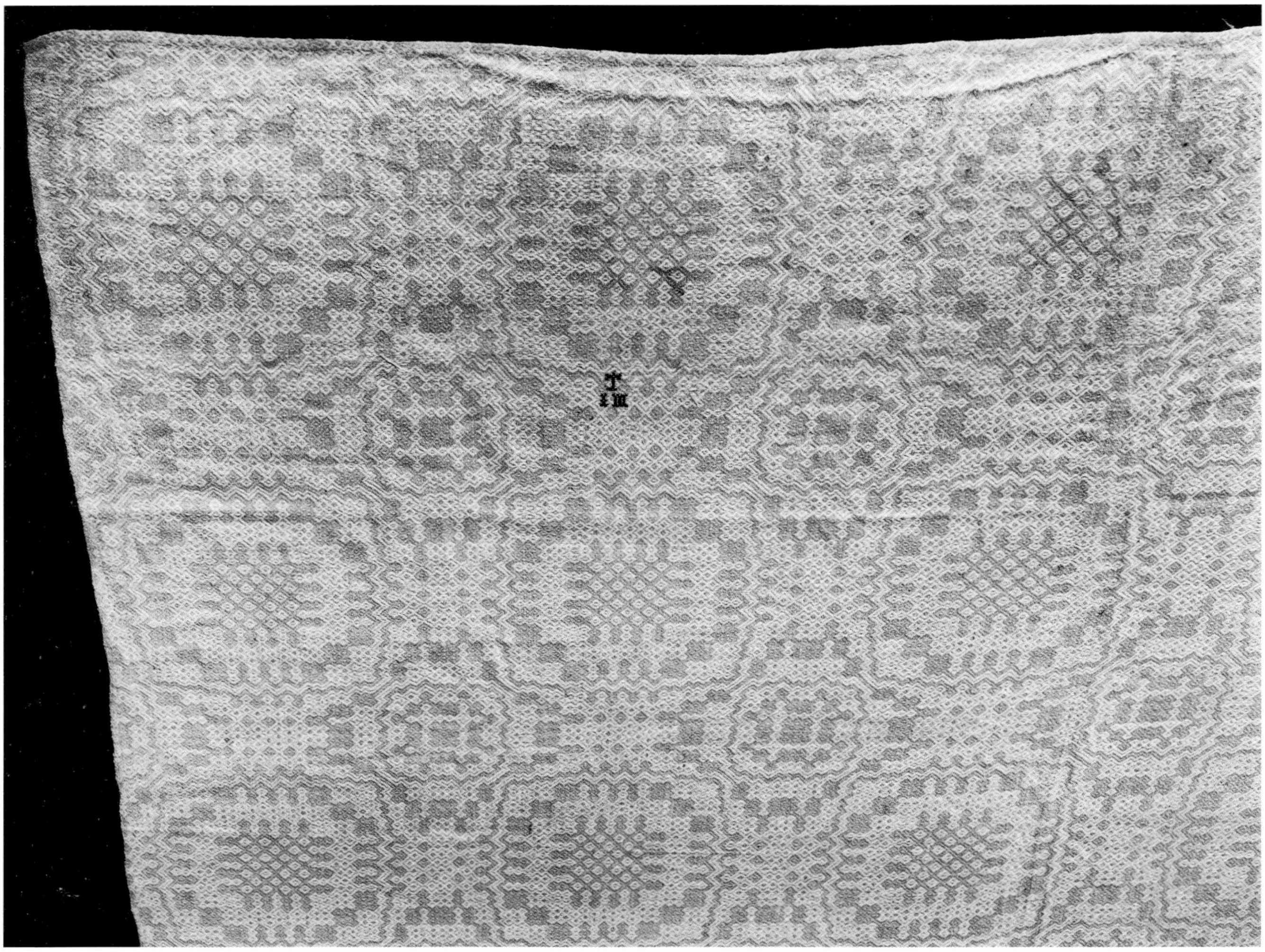

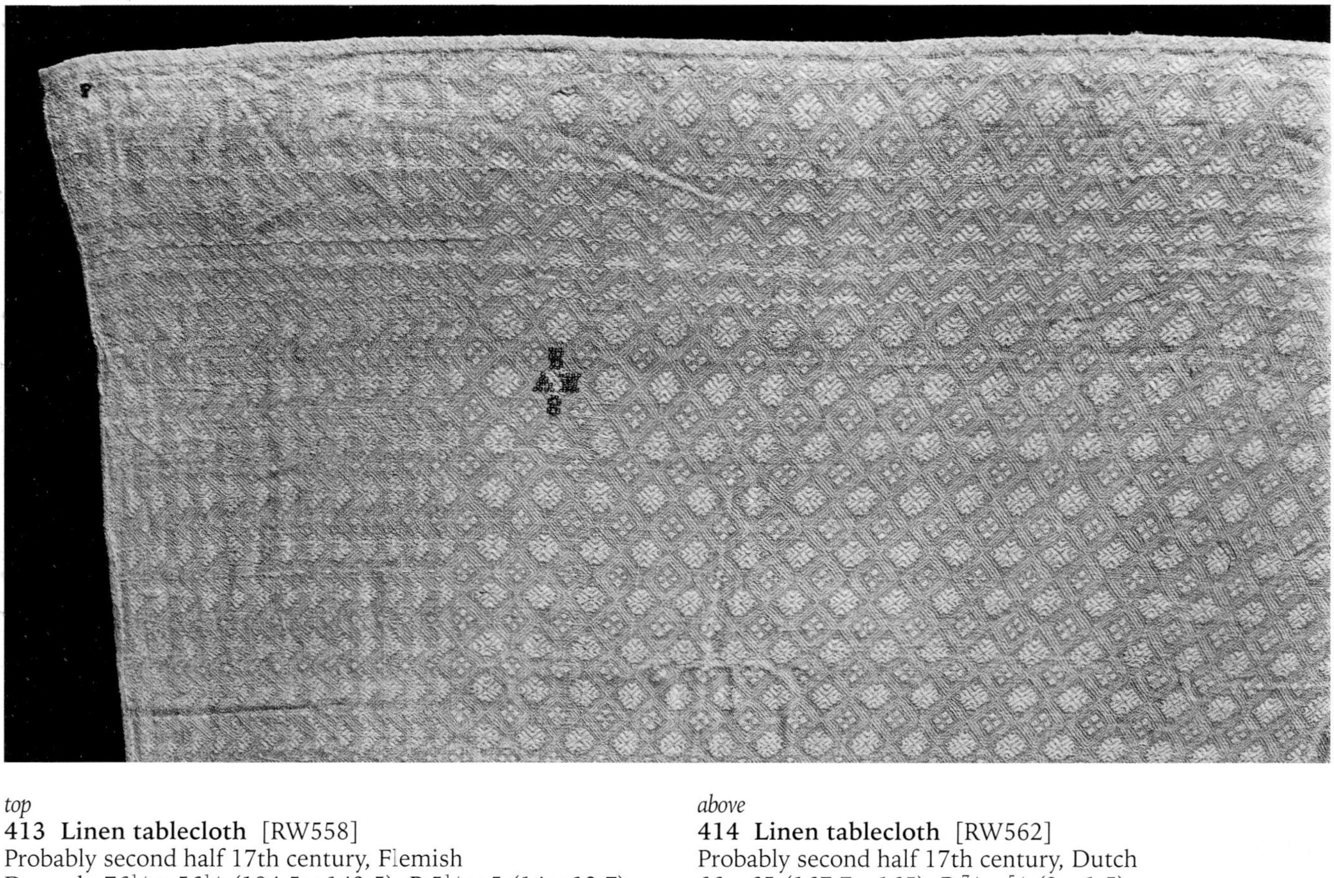

top
413 Linen tablecloth [RW558]
Probably second half 17th century, Flemish
Damask. 76½ × 56½ (194.5 × 143.5); P 5½ × 5 (14 × 12.7)
British mark I^{T}M in brown silk, probably black originally.
Pattern is called crossed diamonds or crossed lozenges.
Two napkin widths sewn edge to edge.

above
414 Linen tablecloth [RW562]
Probably second half 17th century, Dutch
66 × 65 (167.7 × 165); P ⅞ × ⅝ (2 × 1.5)
English mark A$^{B}_{8}$W top left, in back stitch,
in faded blue linen thread.

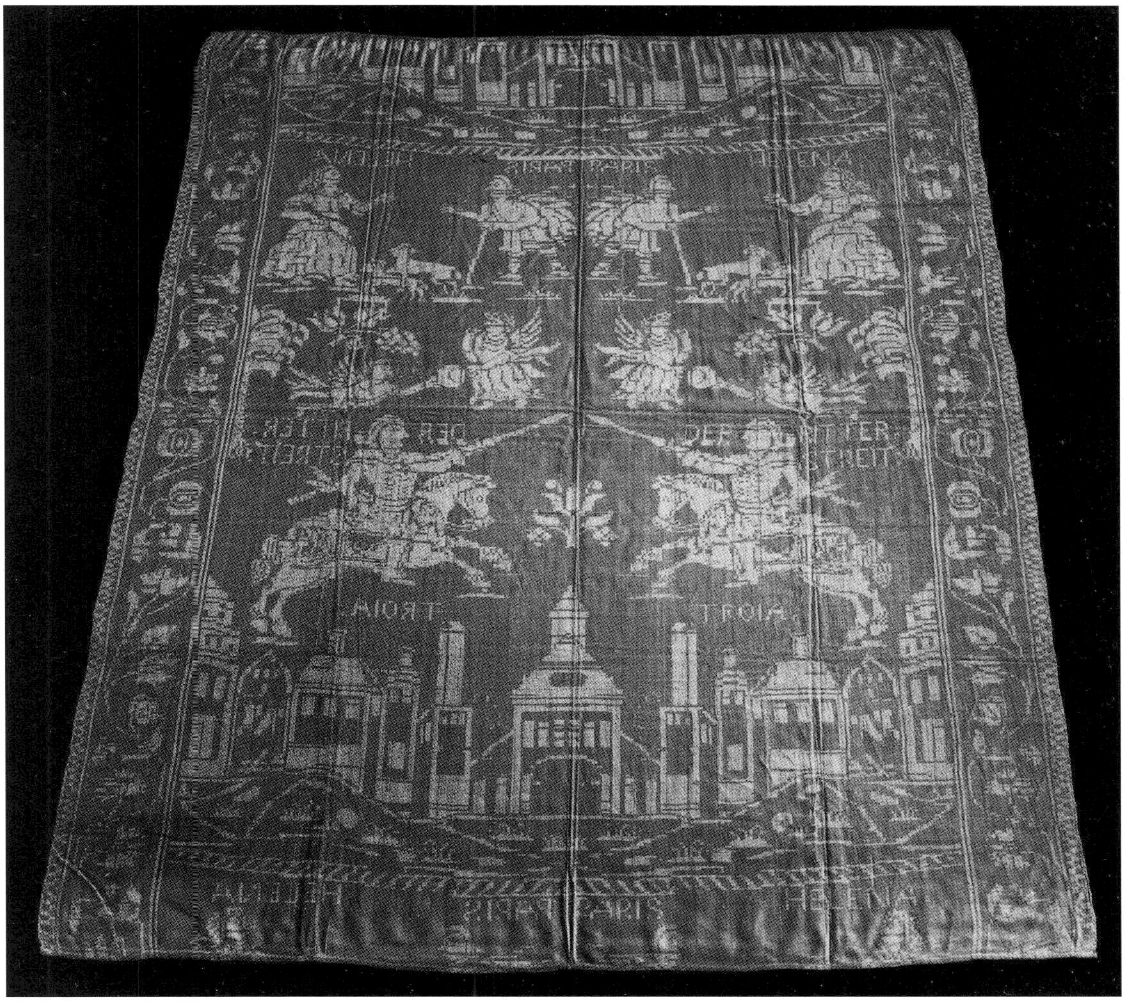

415 Linen cloth [RW561]
1680 to 1700, Saxony, Germany
Damask, satin of 5
36½ × 26½ (92.7 × 67.3); P 28 × 20½ (71 × 52)
Depicts the story of Helen and Paris. Once owned by Martha Tessimond.

416 Linen tablecloth [RW521]
c.1710
Damask
36 × 44 (91.5 × 111.8); P 24½ × 19 (62.3 × 48.2)
Depicting Abraham and Isaac. Initials AO and B.E.A. written in one corner. No borders remaining.
Ex Benjamin Abbott, an ancestor of Roger Warner.

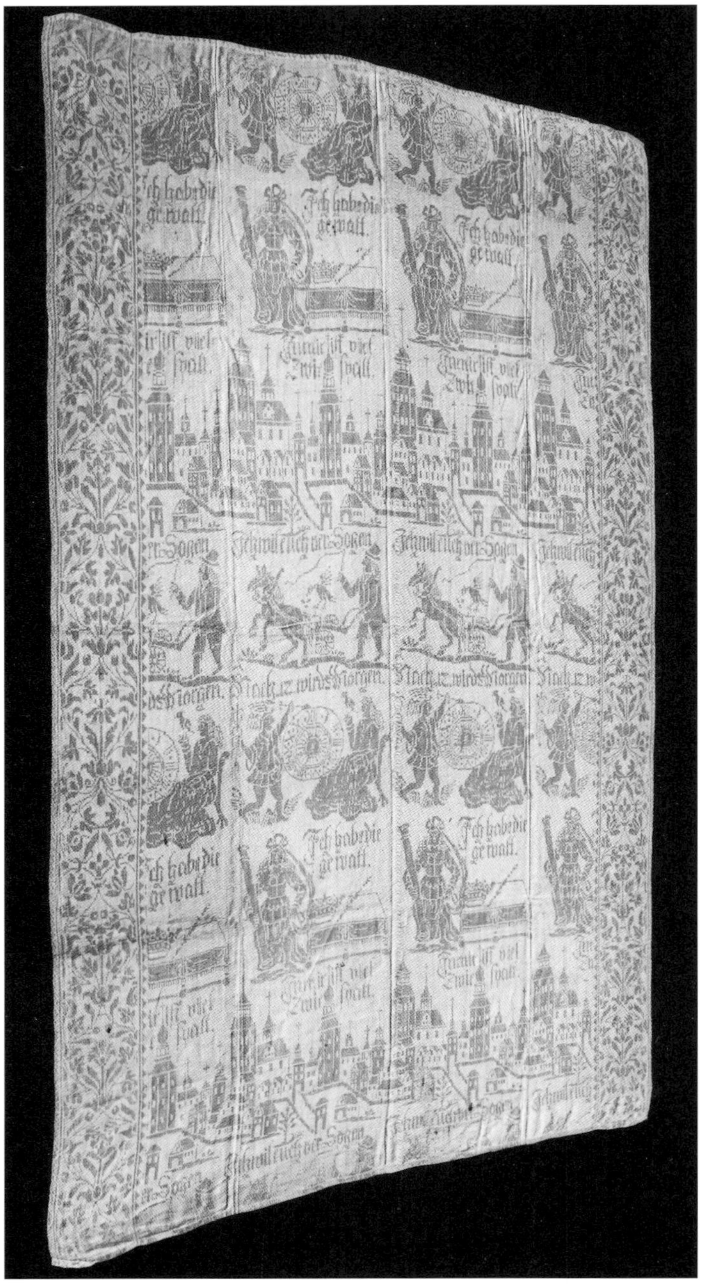

417 Linen napkin [RW560]
c.1720 to 30, Saxony, Germany
Damask, satin of 8
$40\frac{3}{4} \times 30\frac{3}{4}$ (103.5 × 78);
P $22\frac{5}{8} \times 23\frac{3}{4}$ (57.5 × 60.3)
Cf. Stedelijk Musea Kortrijk, *Damast 2* (Kortrijk, 1996), Cat. no. 225; G.T. Van Ysselsteyn, *White Figurated Linen Damask* (The Hague, 1962), Cat. no. 212.

418 Linen napkin [RW555]
c.1730, possibly Scottish
Damask
$40 \times 31\frac{1}{2}$ (101.5 × 80);
P $5\frac{1}{4} \times 4\frac{1}{2}$ (13.3 × 11.5)
English owner's mark $w^{K}m$ embroidered in 'Coventry blue' linen thread in cross stitch.

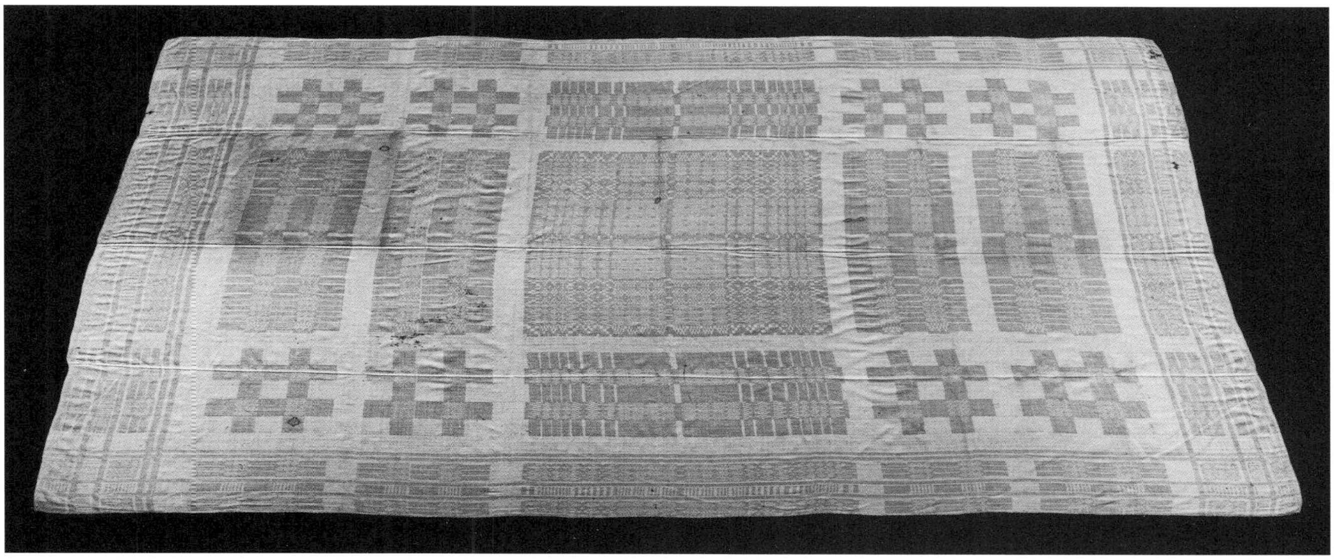

above
419 Linen napkin [RW556]
c.1770 to 80, British
Damask
43¼ × 29¾ (110 × 75.5)
English owner's mark w^{K}m embroidered in 'Coventry blue' linen thread.

left
420 Linen napkin [RW559]
c.1800, English, probably Lancashire or Yorkshire
Deformed tabby (huckaback)
30½ × 26½ (77.5 × 67.3)
Marked BS in blue, top right corner, probably for Bartholemew Smith who married Harriet Tessimond.

below
421 Linen luncheon napkin [RW557]
Second half 19th century, British
Damask
33 × 22¾ (84 × 58); P 3¾ × 1½ (9.5 × 3.8)
Retains the original dressing applied by the manufacturers.

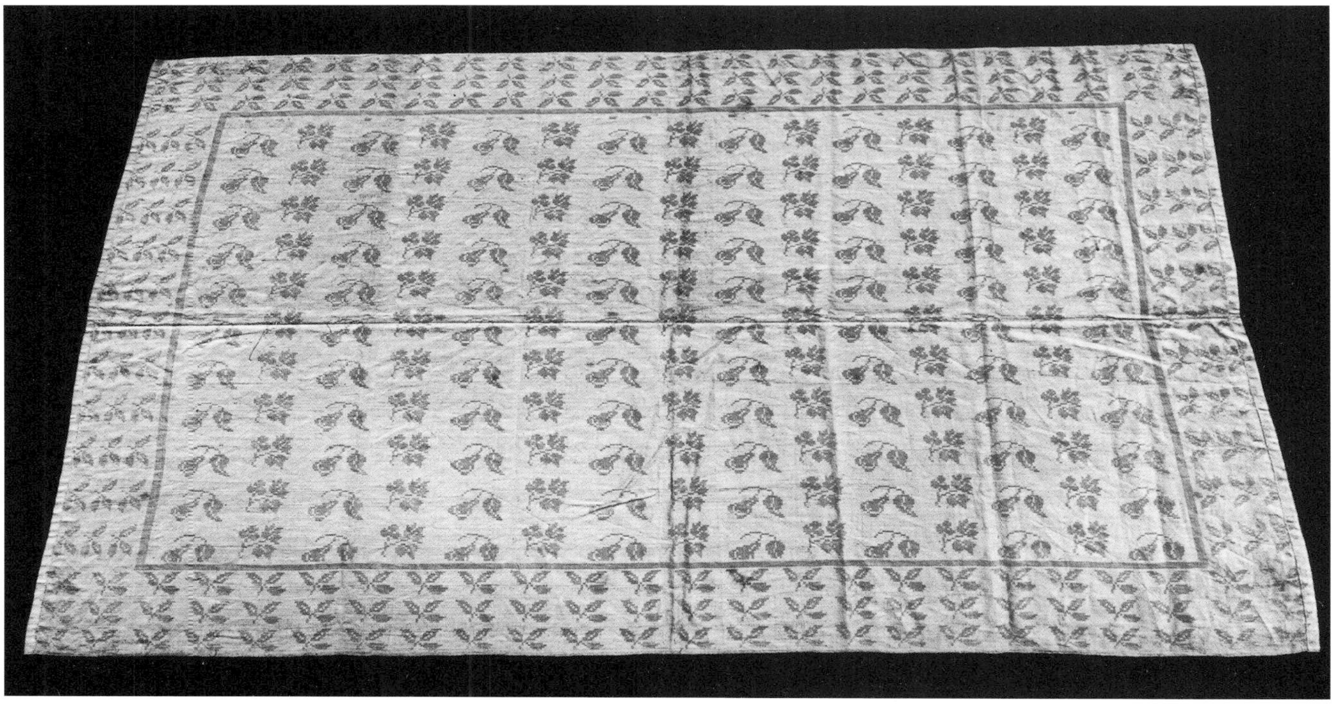

left
422 Furnishing linen [RW266]
Late 19th century
Complex weave
w. 54 (137.1); P 10½ × 7½
(26.7 × 19.7)
Bolt end of white linen with woven pattern on one side only of lattice filled bands alternating with meandering leaves.

below
423 Linen napkins, set of 3
[RW575]
Late 19th century
Damask
29 × 27 (73.7 × 68.5)
Designed by Lewis F. Day.
Marked ?G. M. Warner.

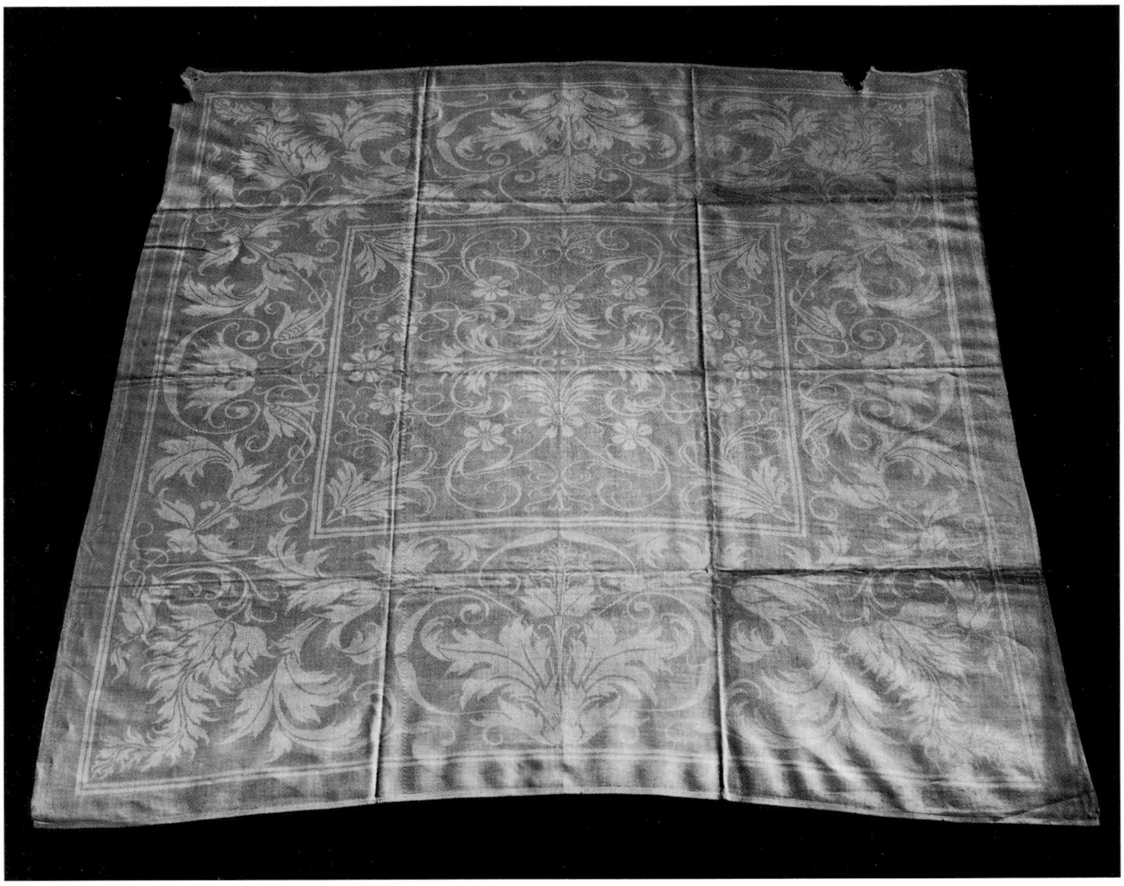

Unillustrated textiles

424 Silk damask [RW13], 1730s, damask, 57 × 20 (145 × 51), P 18.25 × 10 (46.5 × 25.5). Same as RW14 (Cat. no. 107).

425 Woven silk [RW33], 19th C, damask, 44 × 22½ (112 × 57) loom width; P 19½ × 10⅜ (49.5 × 26.3)

426 Furnishing cotton [RW42], second half 19th C, damask, 6½ × 25¼ (16.5 × 65); P ? × 26 (66)

427 Woven silk [RW59], 19th C, 26 × 9 (66 × 23), 26¾ (68). Same as RW58 (Cat. no. 15).

428 Dress silk [RW67], 1790s, complex weave, 18½ × 3½ (47 × 8.9); P 5¾ × 7 (14.6 × 17.8). Same as RW66 (Cat. no. 56).

429 Woven silk [RW73], late 19th or early 20th C, Japanese, complex weave, 17¼ × 22½ (43.8 × 56.8); P 7½ × 3½ (19 × 8.8)

430 Brocaded silk [RW75], 1730s, 15 × 13 (38.2 × 33), P 10¾ (27.3)

431 Brocaded silk [RW76], 1730s, 6 × 5 (25.2 × 12.7)

432 Brocaded silk [RW77], early 18th C, 5½ × 4 (14 × 10.2)

433 Brocaded silk [RW79], early 18th C, 7¼ × 5¼ (18.4 × 13.3). Part of a maniple. Same as RW78 (Cat. no. 11).

434 Brocaded silk [RW87], 1730s, 5½ × 8¾ (14 × 22.2)

435 Brocaded silk [RW90], mid 18th C

436 Brocaded silk [RW98], mid 18th C, 6½ × 5¾ (16.5 × 14.6)

437 Silk and linen brocatelle [RW113], mid 18th C, 58 × 25 (147.3 × 63.5); P 29 × 24⅝ (73.7 × 62.3)

438 Silk and linen brocatelle [RW116, 117], first half 18th C, 11 × 26 (28 × 6).

439 Woven wool [RW124], date uncertain, tabby weave, 57 × 63 (145 × 160)

440 Wool and cotton furnishing [RW126], late 19th C, complex weave, 16 × 34 (40.7 × 86.4); P 20½ × 11½ (52 × 29.2). Machine-woven to give the effect of needlework.

441 Printed cotton, 5 joined pieces [RW143], early 19th C, probably French, copper-plate printed, 11¾ × 24½ (29.8 × 62.2)

442 Printed cotton [RW152], c.1837, block-printed, with roller-printed ground,

22½ × 6 (57.2 × 15.3); P 9¼ × 8½ (23.5 × 21.6). Stead McAlpin, same as RW151 (Cat. no. 290)

443 Printed cotton [RW210], 1835 to 50, block and roller-printed, 28 × 25 (71 × 63.5) loom width; P 12 × 18½ (30.5 × 47), same as RW209 (Cat. no. 288).

444 Printed cotton [RW235], 11 × 28 (27.9 × 71.2), P 4½ × 9 (11.4 × 22.8)

445 Printed cotton curtain [RW242, 243], late 19th C, block-printed, 31 × 21 (79 × 53.4), P 14½ × 32 (36.3 × 81.3), same as RW241 (Cat. no. 342).

446 Printed cotton [RW245, 247], 1883, block-printed, 3 × 15½ (7.5 × 39.4); P 9¼ × 12 (23.5 × 30.5), *Wey*, William Morris, 1883. Same as RW246 (Cat. no. 336).

447 Printed cotton curtain [RW250], late 19th century, block-printed, 98 × 26½ (249 × 67.3), P 16½ × 8¾ (42 × 22.3)

448 Linen furnishing [RW259], checked tabby weave, 17 × 17 (43.2 × 43.2); P 1¼ × 1 (2.5 × 3)

449 Linen furnishing [RW260], second half 18th C, checked tabby weave, 24 × 17½ (61 × 44.5); P 1 × 1¼ (2.5 × 3.2). Edged with blue and white checked tape.

450 Linen furnishing [RW261], second half 18th C, checked tabby weave, 15 × 7½ (38.1 × 19); P 1 × 1¼ (2.5 × 3.2)

451 Cotton furnishing [RW260.1], 1770s, complex weave, 17 x ¾ (43.2 × 1.9). Tape often used for trimming case covers, Cf. F. Montgomery, *Textiles in America* pl.D.36a

452 Linen furnishing [RW262], second half 18th C, checked tabby weave 17¼ × 65 × 3 (43.8 × 165 × 7.6); P 3 × 2¾ (7.6 × 7) sofa squab cover

453 Metal strip and thread on cotton [RW268], second half 19th to early 20th C, Greek Island, of Turkish influence, double-sided work in satin, stem and darning stitches, 28½ × 21 (70 × 52) loom width

454 Worsted on fustian [RW272], early 18th C, coral, herringbone and encroaching satin stitches, 7 × 56 (17.8 × 142.2) loom width 19 (48.3); P ? × 18½ (47), fragment of bed furniture from Cusworth Hall, Doncaster

455 Silk on cotton [RW275], 15 × 20 (38.1 × 50.8). 1720s to 30s, Indian. Hooked needle, or *ari*, work. Same as RW504 (Cat. no. 385).

456 Worsted on linen [RW280], mid 18th C, upright Gobelin stitch, 23 × 33 (58.5 × 84); P 15¾ × 12½ (40 × 32). Used to upholster a chair seat.

457 Printed cotton [RW281], 19th C ?, roller-printed. Length of pink and white striped glazed cotton, still on the roll.

458 Woven cotton [RW282], 19th C, tabby, w. 26 (66), four varying lengths of bright yellow glazed cotton.

459 Glazed cotton banner [RW283], 19th C, tabby weave, w. 26½ (67.3). Length of pink glazed cotton, onto which are glued Gothick-style letters cut out of white cotton, spelling the motto BY INDUSTRY WE PROSPER.

460 Cotton velvet [RW286], 19th C ?, cut pile, 37 × 11 (94 × 28)

461 Cotton velvet [RW287–289], 19th C ?, 2¾ × 39⅜ (7 × 100) loom width 27½ (70). Cut warp pile of deep pink, ground warp and weft pale pink.

462 Silk velvet [RW290–293], 18th C ?, RW290 is 4 × 10⅝ (10 × 27); fragments of striated rose pink cut pile, paler warp and weft. Selvedge yellow with two green stripes.

463 Silk velvet [RW294], 18th C ?, 15⅜ × 2⅜ (39 × 6), striated red cut pile

464 Silk velvet [RW295–6], 18th C ?, fragments of chair upholstery, RW296 is 29⅛ × 13⅜ (74 × 34).

465 Silk velvet [RW298–299], 18th C ?, cut pile, RW298 is 22½ × 19¾ (57 × 50); fragments of egg shell blue, selvedge of twill weave, in red and yellow stripes.

466 Silk velvet [RW300–3], 18th C ?, fragments with fabric width 20½ (52). Egg shell blue velvet with cut silk pile, narrow yellow and white selvedge. Signs of glue, and nail holes.

467 Silk velvet [RW304–305], 18th C ?, fabric width 21⅝ (55). Egg shell blue velvet with cut silk pile, quite worn; green selvedge.

468 Silk velvet [RW308–310], 18th C ?, 50 × 35 (55.5 × 76), cut silk velvet, dark forest green, selvedge narrow with three white stripes; machine-seamed. Formerly chair seat cover – each corner is cut away to fit round legs.

469 Silk velvet [RW311], 18th C ?, 22 × 9 (56 × 23), black silk cut pile velvet, with narrow hand-sewn seam, cut in curved shape, once seamed around the edge.

470 Worsted furnishing [RW313], second half 19th C, cut pile velvet, stamped, 15⅜ × 17¼ (39 × 44)

471 Gold furnishing lace [RW315], second half 18th C, bobbin lace made with gold filé, 18 × ⅝ (46 × 1.5). This simple fan pattern was used throughout the 18th C.

472 Silk and linen brocatelle [RW318], second half 19th C, 29½ × 16 (75 × 40.7)

473 Silk and linen damask [RW322], early 18th C ?, 9½ × 10½ (24 × 26.6), red silk weft-faced Baroque design, same as RW321 (Cat. no. 96).

474 Silk and linen brocatelle [RW327, 328], 18th C, 18 × 10 (45.7 × 25.4), 2 pieces shaped to upholster the wing of a chair. Same as RW329 (Cat. no. 147).

475 Silk and linen brocatelle [RW331, 332], 5 × 13 (12.7 × 33), upholstery tacks remain in the edge, which is strengthened with heavy linen tape. Selvedge on one side.

476 Silk and linen brocatelle [RW333], first half 18th C, 7½ × 12 (19 × 30.5)

477 Woven linen and silk furnishing [RW341–345], 19th C ?, linen weft, silk warp; herringbone and satin weaves, P width 9¼ (23.5).

478 Furnishing silk [RW349.1], mid 19th C, damask, 58 × 64½ (147.4 × 163.8); P 37 × 27¼ (94 × 69.2)

479 Silk and cotton damask [RW350], late 19th C, silk warp, cotton weft; machine-sewn. Damask pattern is 18th C. Same as RW351 (Cat. no. 126).

480 Woven silk [RW352], 18th or 19th C, satin weave, 6¼ × 13⅜ (16 × 34)

481 Woven silk [RW353], satin, 6¼ × 13⅜ (16 × 34). Small silk satin fragment of crimson colour.

482 Dress silk [RW354], 17th to 18th C, tabby weave with fine stripes in warp, 35¾ × 8 (90 × 20), two selvedges, flat-seamed together. Typical of dress and furnishing silks relying either on weave structure or variations of colour in the warps or wefts.

483 Silk and cotton furnishing [RW362], 19th C, complex weave brocaded with gilt filé with a high copper content, 16 × 17½ (40.6 × 44.4). Originally part of a large patterned wall panel in an 18th C style.

484 Woven silk [RW364], 18th C, complex weave with brocading, 16½ × 13 (42 × 33), various samples.

485 Painted silk [RW367, 368], late 18th C. Pieces of a dress

486 Worsted furnishing [RW372], mid 19th C, damask, 22 × 52 (57 × 132) loom width 26 (66); P ? × 26 (66). Two widths hand-sewn together with flat seam.

487 Worsted furnishing [RW381], mid 19th C, damask, 37 × 11¾ (92 × 30); P 26 (65.5) × ?. Pattern same as RW373 (Cat. no. 170).

488 Silk furnishing [RW382], 19th C, complex weave, 7½ × 1½ (20 × 3.5); P 1 × 1⅜ (2.5 × 3.5). Fragment of ribbon of type used for trimming curtains in 19th C.

489 Wool on canvas [RW390], 18th C, tabby weave with linen and tent stitch 19 × 17½ (48.2 × 44.5)

490 Worsted furnishing [RW391], probably mid 18th C, ribbed tabby weave, stamped, 13½ × 28½ (34 × 71) loom width; P ? × 28½ (72.5)

491 Worsted furnishing [RW393], probably 18th C, ribbed tabby weave, watered, 18 × 4½ (47 × 11). One selvedge.

492 Worsted furnishing [RW395], probably 18th C, ribbed tabby weave, watered, 10 × 26¾ (25 × 68)

493 Worsted furnishing [RW396], probably 19th C, tabby weave, 19½ × 14½ (51 × 37.5)

494 Worsted furnishing [RW397], probably 19th C, ribbed tabby weave, watered, diam. 16 (41). Probably upholstery from a round stool.

495 Worsted furnishing [RW398], probably 18th C, tabby weave, glazed, 5½ × 26¾ (14 × 68)

496 Woven linen [RW400–403], possibly 18th C, tabby weave, 14½ × 25½ (37 × 65) loom width

497 Woven silk [RW405], possibly 19th C, tabby weave, 18 × 20 (45 × 50) loom width

498 Worsted furnishing [RW406], probably 18th C, ribbed tabby weave, watered, 3 × 26 (8 × 66) loom width

499 Linen case cover [RW409], plain weave, 19 × 18 (47 × 50), cover, folded to make square, and seamed down opposite edge to fold.

500 Linen furnishing [RW420], early 20th C, damask, 26 × 24 (66 × 62); P 9½ × 4½ (23.5 × 11.5).

501 Wool and silk on wool [RW424], late 19th C, stem, long-and-short, and satin stitches, with French knots, 14 × 25½ (36 × 66); P ? × 14½ (37)

502 Woven silk [RW430–432], 19th C, satin and plain weave in stripes, RW430 is 23⅝ × 21¼ (60 × 54); unpicked from a dress.

503 Silk on linen [RW434,435], 22½ × 56 (56 × 143), 21½ × 22½ (55 × 57)

504 Woven cotton and synthetic [RW446], mid 20th C, complex weave, 32 × 16½ (81.3 × 42); P 3 × 4 (7.6 × 10). Piece roughly made up into curtain.

505 Printed cotton [RW473], 20th C, roller-printed, 19½ × 34 (49.5 × 86.4) loom width

506 Silk on silk [RW505], 1820s to 30s, stem and long-and-short stitches, French knots, 14 × 17¼ (36.2 × 43.8)

507 Silk and metal on silk [RW506], 20th C?, cut pile velvet with appliqued tabby silk and couched metal thread, 9½ × 6½ (24.1 × 16.5). Probably a faked antique fragment.

508 Silk and Japanese gold thread on worsted [RW511], 1890s, satin stitch, laid-and-couched work, 11 × 9 (27.9 × 22.8), western imitation of Oriental work, probably bought from Liberty's of London by Metford Warner.

509 Worsted on linen canvas [RW514], 18th C, tent stitch and French knots, unfinished, 21 × 17½ (53.3 × 44.5). The tapes were used to mount the work on the embroidery frame. The design would have been drawn by a professional.

510 Cotton on cotton [RW518], c.1800 to 1810, running stitch, 37 × 12 (94 × 30.5); P 5 × 3¼ (12.7 × 8.2). Pieces from a muslin gown.

511 Linen furnishing [RW524], late 19th C, damask, 73 × 73 (185 × 185). Embroidered W in top left hand corner. M. WARNER written in ink on hem.

512 Woven linen [RW528], date uncertain, tabby weave, 46 × 30 1½ (117 × 77.5). Plain linen cloth of heavy weight; one width hemmed at each end.

513 Linen furnishing [RW529], late 19th C, damask, 110 × 74 (279.5 × 188)
Table cloth with two pieces of paper enclosed saying *Owl table cloth made especially for uncle Philip Crowley and Aunt Anna for dinner parties* and *large Owl Warner table cloth.* Embroidered W in corner.

514 Worsted furnishing [RW544], 19th C, damask, 9 × 26 (23 × 66) loom width; P 31¾ × 24⅜ (80.2 × 61.9)

515 Worsted wool [RW545], date unknown, ribbed tabby weave, watered, 16½ × 12¼ (42 × 31.5)

516 Worsted wool [RW546], date unknown, ribbed tabby weave, watered, 138¾ × 26½ (352.5 × 67.3)

517 Album of embroidered samples [RW548], many East European, various techniques. Collected by Alice Armes of Burford, 20th C, first half.

518 Printed cotton [RW554], 20th C, roller-printed, 96 × 128 (243.9 × 325) loom width 32 (81.3); P 5 × 6½ (2.7 × 16.5)

519 Linen damask napkin [RW563], 19th C, 19½ × 20 (49.5 × 51). Cut from edge of tablecloth and hemmed on three sides.

520 Bolster case [RW564], c.1852, 18 × 56 (46 × 142); two widths sewn selvedge to selvedge, embroidered in cross-stitch in red A 1 H

521 Linen length [RW565], 19th C, 148½ × 28½ (377 × 72.5)

522 Linen sheet [RW566], 102 × 80 (259 × 204), embroidered A.H / 1 / 1852 in cross-stitch in red.

523 Linen sheet [RW567], 1852; 102 × 80 (259 × 204), embroidered as RW566

524 Linen sheet [RW568], probably early 18th C, 165 × 86 (419 × 218.5), embroidered W K M / 3 in blue.
Two widths sewn selvedge to selvedge.

525 Coarse linen sheet [RW569], probably 18th C, 103½ × 74 (263 × 204). Two widths sewn flat, selvedge to selvedge.

526 Printed cotton [RW570], 19th C, huswife

527 Fragment of quilted worsted [RW571], glazed, 37 × 12 (94 × 30.5), paper label: M. Tessimond.

528 Furnishing worsted [RW576], 19th C, damask, worsted and cotton
13¾ × 16¼ (34.9 × 41.3); P ? × 25½ (? × 64.8)

529 Coarse linen length [RW577], probably 18th C., 93½ × 33 (237.5 × 84); hemmed both ends.

530 Fragment of linen 'Jim-jam' curtain [RW578], 35 × 46 (89 × 117); bought c.1900 at Liberty by Metford Warner, originally used to protect a Caucasian rug in transit.

Glossary

Terms used in the text and captions

Arabesque Flowing overall pattern of small stylised stems and leaves, derived during the Renaissance from Islamic ornament.

Baize A heavy woollen fabric, felted and usually raised or napped on both sides.

Block-printed A method of printing on fabric using one or more wooden blocks, carved in relief with the whole or part of the pattern, depending on the number of colours to be printed. Fine detail could be achieved by inserting metal strips and pins into the surface of the block. Blocks were 'registered' one over another by means of pins hammered into the corners. Fabrics were printed with dyes or more often with the mordants that bond the dyes to the cloth; the principal mordants – alum, iron and tin – produce different colours when the fabric is dipped into the same dye-bath.

Bourette Silk textile with a weft of *bourette,* a thick yarn carded and spun from the coarse outer fibres of cocoons.

Brocade Additional weft bound into the main weave of a textile and used to form a pattern. Because of the cost of gold and silver thread and silk itself, brocading wefts do not stretch from selvedge to selvedge but cover only the area of pattern required. In the 18th century the term brocade was used for a textile – not necessarily but most often of silk – patterned in this way. Nowadays the term is loosely applied to patterned silk.

Brocatelle A strong furnishing fabric resembling silk *damask* in appearance. It is warp-faced so the main weft of linen, jute or cotton is hidden by the silk warp and pattern weft. The warp is sometimes tensioned so the pattern appears slightly raised.

Calendered Finish applied to the surface of textile by machine combining moisture, heat and pressure.

Chalice veil Square of fabric used to cover a chalice or communion cup.

Chasuble The principal vestment worn by the priest for the celebration of the Mass. Usually decorated with *orphreys* on back and front.

Chinoiserie European use of Chinese or pseudo-Chinese motifs in pattern or design.

Complex weave Term used here to describe structures (other than brocade, brocatelle and damask) which employ either more than one set of warps and/or wefts, or more than one weave structure, or occasionally both.

Copper-plate printed Printing technique employing one or more engraved copper plates, up to 36 inches square, in which the plates were inked and then rubbed clean. The dye or mordant remained only in the engraved lines and was transferred to the textile under pressure. This 'intaglio' technique was made possible by the invention in Ireland in 1752 of thickeners enabling dyes and mordants to be printed; by the early 19th century copper-plate printing was generally replaced by machines printing from engraved rollers.

Cotton Yarn spun from the fibrous covering of the seed of the cotton plant; fabric woven from cotton yarn. Cotton first came into Europe from Egypt and the eastern Mediterranean, then India, and finally America, where it had been introduced by settlers. In late-mediaeval Britain, the term Cotton denoted coarse woollens woven in the Manchester area and in north Wales, where *fustians* of wool and linen were also made. During the 16th century imported cotton fibre began to be spun in the same areas, where it replace the wool in fustian and the name was transferred. To protect the wool and silk industries, the weaving of all-cotton fabric was prohibited in England from the opening years of the 18th century, except for export. Printed goods for domestic sale had to be fustian. Changes in fashion, which forced the lifting of the ban in 1774, favoured the use of printed cottons.

Cut pile See *Velvet*

Damask A self-patterned reversible fabric with a single warp and weft; the design is formed by the contrasting warp and weft faces of the same weave, usually satin. Damasks were woven in linen, silk, worsted and cotton for table linen, clothing and furnishings.

Dimity Cotton dress and furnishing fabric patterned in the weave, most often with stripes but also with diamonds, flowers and other small figures.

Drugget Originally an open-weave textile of wool, or a mixture of wool and silk or linen; by c.1825 the term was increasingly used to describe a textile designed to cover a carpet in daily use or occasionally a printed felt used as a floor-covering or carpet underlay.

Embossed The term is mainly used to describe the technique of decorating a fabric by passing it through heated rollers made of wood or metal and carved or engraved with a pattern. The technique was usually employed to make a less expensive fabric – such as a worsted *moreen* – imitate a more costly one; but it was also used to pattern expensive velvets made of silk or worsted.

Filé Flat strip of gold or silver-gilt, wound onto a straight thread usually of silk. This is the most usual type of gold and silver thread, and contrasts with *frisé* and with flat metal (see *lamé*) or metal wire which were also used.

Frisé Flat strip of gold or silver-gilt, wound onto a spiral thread usually of silk, producing a crinkled effect which catches the light and gives extra sparkle.

Fustian A mixed fabric, in the mediaeval period of linen and wool, from the 16th century onwards of linen and cotton. Until the early 16th century it was imported into England but fustians were being woven in Norfolk by the second half of the century and subsequently in the Manchester area using imported cotton.

Glazed Shiny surface effect achieved by passing a fabric between two plain heated rollers under pressure. Often used on worsteds and printed cottons.

Grotesque Type of design based on antique Roman wall and ceiling paintings in the Golden Palace of Nero, excavated from c.1480. Grotesques were very popular amongst Renaissance-Revival designers of the late 19th century.

Harateen A worsted furnishing fabric related to *moreen* and most popular during the first half of the 18th century; dyed red, green, yellow or blue, it was a speciality of Norwich and is characterised by having coarser weft yarns than warps. Harateen has a wavy pattern – created by folding the fabric lengthwise and passing it between heated copper rollers under great pressure – sometimes with additional linear pattern achieved by means of an engraved roller. Remey George, 'Upholder', supplied Rich, 5th Viscount Irwin of Temple Newsam, with a crimson damask bed and matching seat-furniture '& false cases [loose covers] to them made of Crimson haratine' in 1718. By the late 18th century harateen was also made in Yorkshire. The 1808 inventory of Temple Newsam describes window curtains of harateen, and harateen bed-furniture (hangings) of green or yellow in servants' rooms.

Jacquard A mechanism attached to a loom, invented c.1801 by Joseph-Marie Jacquard (1752–1834), which automatically raised the warp threads on a loom. Employing wire needles and a series of punched cards, it eliminated the need for a drawboy who hitherto manipulated the warp cords.

Lamé Term used to describe a weave including silver or silver-gilt thread, usually in the form of metal strip. It may also be called plate.

Linen Cloth made from flax in many different weaves and grades. England imported linen goods from Ireland, the Netherlands, France and other northern European countries.

Maniple A narrow strip of material worn over the left forearm by priests during the celebration of the Mass.

Moreen Worsted cloth with coarse weft yarns, related to *harateen*. It usually has a watered figure on one side achieved by folding the cloth randomly and passing it between rollers under great pressure. Its name apparently derives from the French word *moiré*, itself a corruption of the English term, mohair. Most popular in the early 18th century when its manufacture centred on Kidderminster in Worcestershire, moreen was revived c.1811 and was made chiefly in Yorkshire. At Temple Newsam in 1808, moreen was used for window curtains and for the furniture (hangings) of beds; green, blue, crimson, 'flesh coloured' and 'drab' all appear. William Farmborough invoiced Temple Newsam for 'a Mohog'y Field Bedstead with Pea Green furniture of Morein' on 3 January 1773, at a cost of £7.

Ornament d'église Silk textile made in France specifically for use in church.

Orphrey Decorative bands, either woven or embroidered, applied to vestments; down the front edges of copes and the centre front and back of *chasubles*. The back orphrey is often cross shaped.

Pencilled Drawn or painted by hand with a fine brush. Sometimes patterns were completely pencilled, both outlines and blocks of colour: sometimes the outlines were block-printed and blocks of colour pencilled afterwards.

Purl Metal strip coiled like a spring and used in embroidery both as straight lengths and as tiny spots.

Rep General term for any fabric with a ribbed effect, resulting for instance from the use of a thicker weft than warp threads. Rep was commonly used for curtains and upholstery.

Roller-printed Machine-printing on fabric using engraved metal or carved wooden rollers. Invented during the 1780s, the technique by 1790 enabled fabric to be printed in four colours at a single pass through the machine. The technique became almost universal during the first half of the 19th century. Around 1805 a machine was produced that could combine metal and wooden rollers, enabling fine outlines and areas of solid colour to be printed virtually simultaneously. Before c.1815 the diameter of the rollers restricted the size of the pattern repeat.

Satin A fabric characterised by having warp threads which float over five or seven wefts and are bound in a broken-twill so that the smooth surface is not visibly interrupted.

Screen-printing A form of stencil printing through an open mesh, areas of which have been stopped out to form a pattern.

Selvedge A narrow band down the edge of a length of fabric woven either with warp threads set more closely together or of a different thickness to those of the centre. Selvedges provided a strong, straight edge and the use of different colours and widths was a means of distinguishing varying qualities of cloth in Italian and other silk industries.

Silk Cloth woven from the shiny filaments produced by the silkworm. The main centre of production in 18th century France was Lyons; its equivalent in England was Spitalfields, on the outskirts of London. Fashionable dress silks came out in new patterns twice a year; patterns for furnishing silks were much more conservative, many remaining in production over very long periods.

Stamped Method of impressing a pattern on a woven fabric by passing it between wooden rollers and a heated brass cylinder engraved with a design.

Stomacher A panel, often stiffened and usually decorated, worn from the late 16th century to the late 18th to fill the space between the straight edges of an open robe from breast to waist.

Tabby Plain weave fabric in which the warp and weft threads interlace at right angles in a regular over-one under-one sequence. In an extended tabby, pairs of warps and wefts pass in the same sequence, while an unbalanced tabby has warps and wefts of different densities but still passing the same way.

Trapunto A form of quilting in which mainly linear patterns are back-stitched in parallel lines through two layers of fabric. Cords or fine rolls of cotton-wool padding are then pushed between the lines of stitches through holes in the thin backing fabric to form a raised pattern on the front. Also known as Italian quilting.

Twill A kind of weave producing a diagonal effect in the finished textile. More elaborate effects could also be achieved, such as diamond or herringbone patterns.

Valance A piece of drapery attached to an object to conceal its structure. Four-post bedsteads, for instance, usually had outer and inner valances around the canopy where they hid the curtain rails and valances screening the frame of the bed itself, giving a total of nine valances in all.

Velvet A fabric with a second warp woven over wires to form loops which can be left uncut or cut to form a pile surface. Voided patterns revealing the ground weave are formed by taking the second warp to the back of the fabric for the desired distance. Velvets can be woven with any fibre.

Vermicular Meandering pattern somewhat resembling worm-tracks.

Voided See *Velvet*

Warp Threads running lengthwise in a loom, crossed by the weft threads to form the textile. The warp threads are usually twisted more tightly than those of the weft.

Watered A decorative effect produced on a textile usually with heavier weft threads than warp. The cloth is folded on itself and submitted to heavy pressure – or wound on rollers and rolled under a heavy weight – resulting in a wavy, watered figure.

Weft Threads of a textile that cross the warp threads at right angles and are interlaced with them to produce a woven cloth.

Wool Short-staple fibres of sheep's wool woven and fulled (shrunk) to produce a dense, heavy fabric.

Worsted Long-staple woollen yarn, woven into a lightweight cloth. The name derives from the town of Worstead near Norwich in Norfolk where much was woven.

Notes on firms and designers

Albert & Crocker/Ramm & Crocker
Drapers, of Watling Street, London, supplied by Bannister Hall, in which accounts they are first recorded in 1803 as J. Crocker. After various family partnerships they became Jonathan & Albert Crocker in 1846, and in 1891 merged with Charles Ramm when the company became known as Ramm, Son & Crocker, as they are known today. Ramm used, amongst others, the Ramsden Wood printworks at Bury, which was block-printing around 1900, although later changed to screen-printing. When the firm shut down c.1953 the Ramm designs went to Stead McAlpin and Company.

Bannister Hall
Printworks at Higher Walton, near Preston, Lancashire, from 1798 to 1893, famous for block-printed furnishing cottons. The founding partners were Richard Jackson of Chelsea and John Stevenson, a calico printer from Walton. In 1809 they were joined by Charles Swainson who provided financial backing and the driving force and continued to run the firm till 1845, with several different partners. Under him the company (trading as Charles Swainson & Co. 1825–56) became very successful, exporting to New York, Turkey and New South Wales; after Swainson retired in 1845 his son, also Charles, took over, although rather less successfully. (*Dennys* recorded 1849 as a partner.) In 1856 the printworks were bought by a long standing customer Thomas Clarkson (*Clarkson and Turner* recorded 1812–39 as a customer). He owned a shop at 17 Coventry Street, London, selling quality furnishing fabrics, many of which were printed by Bannister Hall; thus the company was known as *Thomas Clarkson & Co.* from 1856 until 1893 when it was bought by *Stead McAlpin & Co.*, at Cummersdale.

Clarkson and Turner
See Bannister Hall

Day, Lewis Foreman (1845–1910)
Son of a Quaker wine-merchant, he trained as stained-glass designer, starting his own business in 1870, mostly for domestic uses. He went on to design wallpapers for, amongst others, Jeffrey & Co., and textiles for Turnbull & Stockdale, becoming their Art Director in 1881. He also designed tiles, furniture and jewellery, and published widely on pattern and ornament design.

Dudding
Oakley, Dudding & Co., recorded as 'furniture printers' at 67 New Bond Street, London from 1802 to 1805. From 1806 to 1811 the firm was Dudding and Nelson but between 1811–1814 just E.B. Dudding appears at 72 New Bond Street, until he was taken over by George Oakley, possibly the same firm as the original partner. Some of their cottons were printed at Bannister Hall.

Gainsborough Silk Weaving Co.
See introduction

Lee, A.H. & Sons
Founded by Arthur Henry Lee (1853–1932) in Warrington in 1888 but moved to Birkenhead in 1904. Produced high quality jacquard-woven wool, silk and cotton furnishing fabrics, using work of leading designers such as Voysey, Crane, and Day. From 1905 they also produced large crewelwork curtains and hangings, but by 1912 they were mostly making reproduction woven fabrics, to suit the fashion. Used Stead McAlpin and Turnbull and Stockdale as printers for cotton fabrics, until the company closed in 1970, when the designs went to Turnbulls.

Miles & Edwards
William Miles, linen-draper, was operating from c.1805 and by 1811 was in Oxford Street, London. In 1806 he had some cottons printed by Bannister Hall. Miles & Edwards, furniture-printers, were active between 1822 and the late 1840s, when they were taken over by Charles Hindley, who continued to produce their most popular designs for several decades.

Morris, William (1834–96)
Known best as an artist and designer, he was also a writer and a socialist. Although he set out as a designer of stained glass, he soon turned to embroideries, tapestries, printed and woven textiles, wallpapers, furniture and books. He established Morris and Company in 1875, although his wallpapers and many woven textiles were made by other companies under licence. He was an extremely knowledgeable textile historian and much of his work shows elements of many different periods of design. He was President of the Arts and Crafts Society in 1893, and was from the beginning a

leading influence on the movement, insisting as he did on traditional craftsmanship, rather than highly mechanised mass-production.

Richard Ovey & Co.
Linen-draper in Covent Garden, active 1790 to 1831, commissioned designs and sent them to outside printworks, especially Bannister Hall, Preston. One of the leading London drapers of the time and supplier to the Royal Family.

Stead McAlpin & Company Ltd.
A calico printworks was founded by Richard and Anthony Halliley in the early 19th century, at Wigton, Cumberland, where they are first recorded in 1828. They were joined in 1832 by Thomas McAlpin (1777–1849 ?) who left in 1834 to establish a printworks at Cummersdale. In 1849, the widowed Mrs McAlpin married Stead, and when the last McAlpin died in 1868, Stead took over the firm, giving it its present name. Long time rivals of the nearby Bannister Hall Printworks, which they bought in 1893 when it ceased trading, acquiring some 9000 designs. One of the earliest firms to use engraved copper rollers, and continued to use block-printing until 1978.

Stonards
Probably drapers, recorded c.1910 to 1956 at 9 Paternoster Buildings, London EC, in Stead McAlpin archive.

Swainson and Dennys
See Bannister Hall.

Voysey, Charles Francis Annesley (1857–1941)
Articled to the architect J.P. Seddon in London in 1874. Set up an independent architectural practice c.1882, which was active until 1920; he also designed a series of basic pieces of furniture. However his interest in surface design developed and from 1883 he designed wallpapers for Jeffrey & Co. (see Introduction), and others, and showed printed fabrics and wallapers at the first exhibition of the Arts & Crafts Exhibition Society in 1888. He became internationally famous for his work, winning the R.I.B.A. Royal Gold Medal in 1940.

Warner & Sons
Silk weaver and cotton printers founded by Benjamin Warner (1828–1908) who trained at Spitalfields School of Design, and in 1870 formed a partnership with Charles Ramm (see above), in which Ramm produced the printed fabrics, and Warner the woven ones. Their premises moved from Spitalfields to Bethnal Green in 1873 and then to Braintree, Essex in 1895; they acquired printworks in Dartford, Kent in the 1920s, enabling them to do their own printing. They traded under various names: Warner, Sillett & Ramm, until 1875; Warner & Ramm (1875–92); Warner & Sons (1892 onwards). They were very well known for traditional floral patterns, but also used avant garde designers such as Owen Jones and Bruce Talbert; noted for high technical achievement, they did not use power-looms until 1919.

Further Reading

This is not a comprehensive bibliography (one can be found, for instance, in Schoeser & Rufey, below) but simply a guide to further information.

Geoffrey Beard, *Upholsterers and Interior Furnishing in England 1530–1840* (New Haven and London, 1997)

Dorothy K. Burnham, *Warp and Weft: A Textile Terminology* (Toronto, 1980)

Pamela Clabburn, *The National Trust Book of Furnishing Textiles* (London, 1988)

Jennifer Harris (ed.), *5000 years of Textiles* (London, 1993)

Wendy Hefford, *The Victoria & Albert Museum's Textile Collection: Design for Printed Textiles in England from 1750 to 1850* (London, 1992)

Monique & Donald King, *European Textiles in the Keir Collection 400 BC to 1800 AD* (London, 1990)

Donald King & Santina M. Levey, *The Victoria & Albert Museum's Textile Collection: Embroidery in Britain from 1200 to 1750* (London, 1995)

Santina M. Levey, *An Elizabethan Inheritance: The Hardwick Hall Textiles* (London, 1998)

Valerie Mendes, *The Victoria & Albert Museum's Textile Collection: British Textiles from 1900 to 1937* (London, 1992)

Florence M. Montgomery, *Printed Textiles: English and American Cottons and Linens, 1700–1850* (New York, 1970)

Florence M. Montgomery, *Textiles in America 1650–1870* (New York, 1984)

Jane C. Nylander, *Fabrics for Historic Buildings* (Washington, 1983)

Linda Parry, *William Morris Textiles* (New York, 1983)

Linda Parry, *Textiles of the Arts and Crafts Movement* (London 1988)

Natalie Rothstein, *Silk Designs of the Eighteenth Century In the Collection of the Victoria and Albert Museum, London* (London, 1990)

Natalie Rothstein, *The Victoria & Albert Museum's Textile Collection: Woven Textile Design in Britain to 1750* (London, 1994)

Natalie Rothstein, *The Victoria & Albert Museum's Textile Collection: Woven Textile Design in Britain from 1750 to 1850* (London, 1994)

Mary Schoeser & Celia Rufey, *English and American Textiles from 1790 to the present* (New York, 1989)

Peter Thornton, *Baroque and Rococo Silks* (London, 1965)

Peter Thornton, *Seventeenth-Century Interior Decoration in England, France and Holland* (New Haven and London, 1978, 1990)

Concordance A

In this list, the Temple Newsam number [RW] is shown in bold type

RW	Cat no.
1	1
2,3	20
4	3
5	121
6	82
7	85
8	83
9	84
10	80
11	90
12	106
13	424
14	107
15	101
16	89
17	91
18	92
19–22	108
23–28	86
29	93
30	102
31	116
32	109
33	425
34	122
35	111
36	78
37	79
38	87
39	94
40	95
41	112
42	426
43	2
44	7
45	4
46	113
47	21
48	22
49	13
50	98
51–53	103
54	14
55–56	118
57	100
58	15
59	427
60	23
61	24
62	117
63	44
64	52
65	45
66	56
67	428
68	57
69	58
70	59
71	74
72	220
73	429
74	16
75	430
76	431
77	432
78	11
79	433
80	12
81	9
82	34
83	19
84	18
85	32
86	25
87	434
88	26
89	33
90	435
91	53
92	46
93	36
94	39
95–6	47
97	27
98	436
99	28
100	40
101	29
102	37
103	54
104	75
105	5
106	136
107	131
108	132
109	135
110	138
111	134
112	137
113	437
114	144
115	139
116–7	438
118	140
119	141
120	142
121	181
122	168
123	214
124	439
125	184
126	440
127	205
128	185
129	372
130	373
132	198
133	199
134	305
135	270
136	222
137	363
138	365
139	239
140	240
141	235
142	237
143	441
144	241
145	238
146	221
147	236
148	250
149	277
150	298
151	290
152	442
153	309
154	297
155–7	271
158–60	272
161	278
162	291
163	280
164	279
165	248
166	357
167	256
168	322
169	300
170	269
171	301
172	254
173	255
174	317
174.1	314
175	344
176	348
177	345
178	346
179	318
180	347
181	302
182	328
183	252
184	349
185	268
186	266
187	325
188	351
189	326
190	267
191	327
192	352
193	320
194	321
195	234
196	310
197	285
198	276
199	282
200	273
201	303
202	359
203	287
204	307
205	358
206	360
207	323
208	251
209	288
210	443
211	245
211.1	244
212	257
213	258
214	259
215	260
216	292
217	261
218	262
219	263
220	293
220.1	294
221	304
222	275
223	306
224	364
225	311
226	329
227	308
228	286
229	264
230	313
231	315
232	289
233	361
234	356
235	444
237	337
238	333
239	334
240	341
241	342
242–3	445
244	354
245,7	446
246	336
248	340
249	338
250	447
251	339
252	355
253	362
254	343
255	353
256	200
257	201
258	195
259	448
260	449
260.1	451
261	450
262	452
263	196
263.1	196
264	202
265	194
266	422
267.1	188
268	453
269	387
270	407
271	375
272	454
273	377
274	374
275	455
276	369
277	386
278	376
279	371
280	456
281	457
282	458
283	459
284	48
285	212
286	460
287–9	461
290–3	462
294	463
295–6	464
297	409
298–9	465
300–03	466
304–05	467
308–10	468
311	469
312	35
313	470
314	215
315	471
316	60
317	153
318	472
319	63
320	367
321–5	96
322	473
326	146
327	474
328	474
329	147
330	148
331–2	475
333	476
334	149
335	150
336	151
337	154
338	176
339	152
340	169
341–5	477
346	49
347	123
348	124
349	478
349.1	125
350	479
351	126
352	480
353	481
354	482
355	8
356	64
357	219
358–60	50
361	17
362	483
363	65
364	484
365	6
366	119
367–8	485
369	190
370	191

371	164
372	486
373	170
374	165
375	166
376	171
377	167
378	172
379	173
380	180
381	487
382	488
383	177
384	174
385	158
386	155
387	155
387.1	155
388	331
389	186
390	489
391	490
392	192
393	491
394	210
395	492
396	493
397	494
398	495
399	211
400–03	496
404	213
405	497
406	498
407	209
408	203
409	499
410	145
411	408
412	388
413	41
414	405
415	175
417	104
418	66
419	206
420	500
420.1	187
421	127
422	115
423a,b	110
424	501
425	312
426	246
427	67
428–32	502
433	381
434–5	503
436	204
437	182
438	218
439	76
440	77
441	133
442	68
443	178
444	128
445	130
446	504
447	81
448	97
449	114
450	62
451	69
452	99
453	105
453.1	183
454	10
455	42
456	70
457	43
458	71
459	55
460	72
461	38
462	73
463	61
464	51
465	249
466	247
467	233
468	253
469	265
470	330
471	284
472	316
473	505
474	319
475	281
476	274
477	224
478a,b	223
478.1	225
479	228
480	226
481	227
482	229
483	230
484	350
485	295
485.1	296
486	332
487	335
488	283
489	207
490	156
491	159
492	160
493	161
494	162
495	179
496	163
497	410
498	378
499	380
500	379
501	392
502	395
503	393
504	385
505	506
506	507
507	366
508	382
509	406
510	398
511	508
512	391
513	389
514	509
515	401
516	404
517	399
518	510
519	400
520	411
521	416
522	412
523	193
524	511
525–7	197
528	512
529	513
530	232
531	299
532	189
533	120
534	390
535	368
536	394
537	30
538	31
539	402
540	403
541	129
542	143
543	88
544	514
544.1	157
545	515
546	516
547	242
548	517
549–50	383
551	384
552	231
553	324
554	518
555	418
556	419
557	421
558	413
559	420
560	417
561	415
562	414
563	519
564	520
565	521
566	522
567	523
568	524
569	525
570	526
571	527
572	216
573	217
574	243
575	423
576	528
577	529
578	530

Concordance B

The present catalogue includes textiles surviving on three chairs given by Roger Warner in the 1980s: this concordance lists their Temple Newsam accession numbers, the numbers under which they appear in this catalogue, and in the third volume of Christopher Gilbert's catalogue of furniture at Temple Newsam and Lotherton Hall published in 1998.

TN no.	**Cat. no.**	**Gilbert 1998**
17/85	370	693
38.1/85	208	698
38.1/85	396	698
63/87	397	700